Matt·
Apr

BFI TV Classics

BFI TV Classics is a series of books celebrating key individual television programmes and series. Television scholars, critics and novelists provide critical readings underpinned with careful research, alongside a personal response to the programme and a case for its 'classic' status.

Civilisation

Jonathan
Conlin

A BFI book published by Palgrave Macmillan

None of the content of this publication is intended to imply that it is endorsed by the programme's broadcaster or production companies involved.

First published in 2009 by
PALGRAVE MACMILLAN

on behalf of the

BRITISH FILM INSTITUTE
21 Stephen Street, London W1T 1LN
www.bfi.org.uk

There's more to discover about film and television through the BFI. Our world-renowned archive, cinemas, festivals, films, publications and learning resources are here to inspire you.

Palgrave Macmillan in the UK is an imprint of Macmillan Publishers Limited, registered in England, company number 785998, of Houndmills, Basingstoke, Hampshire RG21 6XS.

Palgrave Macmillan in the US is a division of St Martin's Press LLC, 175 Fifth Avenue, New York, NY 10010.

Palgrave Macmillan is the global academic imprint of the above companies and has companies and representatives throughout the world.

Palgrave® and Macmillan® are registered trademarks in the United States, the United Kingdom, Europe and other countries.

Set by Cambrian Typesetters, Camberley, Surrey
Printed in China

This book is printed on paper suitable for recycling and made from fully managed and sustained forest sources. Logging, pulping and manufacturing processes are expected to conform to the environmental regulations of the country of origin.

British Library Cataloguing-in-Publication Data
A catalogue record for this book is available from the British Library

ISBN 978–1–84457–270–0

Contents

Acknowledgments

Researching and writing this book has been very enjoyable, and my thanks go first and foremost to Rebecca Barden and the TV Classics' advisory panel, for allowing me to write it, and to the history department of Southampton University, for help with travel and research costs. Liz Cooper and Steve Hilton at Granada Media and especially Kathleen Dickson at the BFI were invaluable in tracking down old programmes. Research in Washington, College Park, New York and elsewhere was made a whole lot easier thanks to help and advice from PBS veteran Jack Caldwell, Ann Neal at Xerox, the National Gallery's Jean Henry and Karen King of the National Public Broadcasting Archives, as well as Martin Gostanian of the Paley Center in LA.

It was a privilege to be able to interview a number of people who knew Kenneth Clark and Michael Gill. All of them made their own contribution to *Civilisation*, and I owe the following a great debt of gratitude for their time, hospitality, photographs, technical information and comments on the manuscript: Sir David Attenborough, Colette Clark, Roger Crittenden, Yvonne Gilan, Georgina Gill, Ken MacMillan, Peter Montagnon, Catherine Porteous and in particular Ann Turner, whose eye for detail is formidable. All responsibility for the views expressed in this book is, however, mine alone. Sophia Contento, Charles Saumarez Smith,

Giles Waterfield, Wim Weymans and John Wyver were extremely helpful as I prepared the manuscript for publication.

Born in New York to British ex-pats, I first watched *Civilisation* when it was re-run on WNET-13 in the 1980s. The series introduced me to European civilisation. So did my uncle, Stephen Conlin. This book is dedicated to him.

1   A Personal View

What is civilisation? I don't know. I can't define it in abstract terms – yet.
But I think I can recognise it when I see it; and I am looking at it now.

Standing on the left bank of the Seine, renowned art historian Kenneth
Clark turns and looks approvingly over the Seine at the cathedral of
Notre Dame. Gothic figures revel in fine tracery, confined but not

He knows it when he sees it

Uncivilised art

constrained by mighty walls and buttresses. A civilised achievement. Yet, Clark continues, somebody standing on the same spot in the 9th century would have been struck by another product of man's art, floating down the river towards him; a symbol of destruction, rather than creativity. To the atonal notes of an organ, we cut to the prow of a Viking ship. 'Looked at today,' Clark notes, 'it's a powerful work of art. But to the mother of a family trying to settle down in her little hut it would have seemed less agreeable – as menacing to her civilisation as the periscope of a nuclear submarine.'

So opened a thirteen-part television series documenting western Europe's creative achievements, from the end of the Dark Ages to Concorde's first flight. Although Michelangelo's David, St Peter's in Rome and other great landmarks appear in the pre-title sequence, once in vision Clark makes it very clear that *Civilisation* is not going to be Clark's Tour of Masterpieces of Western Art. Viewing such great works could, Clark concedes, lead us to believe western European civilisation to be unstoppable. But that would be wrong. 'All the life-giving activities that we lump together under "civilisation" have been obliterated once, when the barbarians ran over the Roman Empire.' Though we just about made it that time, 'in the last few years we've developed an uneasy feeling that it could happen again'. 'Advanced thinkers' have, Clark says, begun to wonder if civilisation is worth preserving. 'Well, this is why it seems to me a good moment to look at some of the ways in which man has shown himself to be an intelligent, creative, orderly and compassionate animal.'

As a presenter Clark's aristocratic authority was leavened by diffidence. He is presenting a thirteen-episode series, but is candid enough to confess an inability to define his subject. Already in the submarine analogy we have an example of those asides whose tangential or throwaway air belies their weight. There would be many more such remarks, equally intent on highlighting parallels between our age, which Clark identified as one of 'Heroic Materialism', and past manifestations of the human spirit in western Europe. *Civilisation* was not going to be a stately progress from darkness to sweetness and light. The enemies of civilisation were ever present, and had a beauty of their own.

Civilisation: A Personal View by Kenneth Clark was commissioned in 1966 by Controller of BBC2 David Attenborough and Head of Programmes Huw Wheldon. Attenborough chose forty-three-year-old Michael Gill as director, who in turn approached Peter Montagnon, a fellow veteran of BBC Schools Television. A third director credit went to Ann Turner, who directed one complete episode as well as the extensive stills sequences that featured in all the others. In 1966 Clark was sixty-three. A privileged background and precocious talents had brought him a series of high-profile jobs in the arts, starting with his appointment as director of the National Gallery. He had gone on to serve as Surveyor of the King's Pictures and chairman of the Arts Council. Experience at the Ministry of Information during World War II introduced Clark to the world of moving pictures. A new career as communicator had begun.

Michael Gill and Clark

4

By 1966 he could have been excused for thinking that he was due for retirement. Although he was sceptical of 'art history' as an academic subject Clark had made a name for himself as the author of books such as *The Nude* (1956) and *Rembrandt and the Italian Renaissance* (1966), which deftly combined intellectual history, philosophy and something we would now recognise as art history. He believed that he only had a certain number of productive years left to him, and wished to focus on his writing. When the BBC first approached him Clark was hesitant. Attenborough and his colleagues worked him over during a lunch at the BBC's flashy new Television Centre. The BBC was eager to show off the possibilities of the high-definition 625-line colour signal that it had introduced in 1967, a marked improvement on the old 405-line standard.

Colour television had enjoyed a head start in the United States, where it had become synonymous with tacky sponsor-driven game shows and Westerns. Attenborough was allocated a budget of a size unprecedented in the BBC's history and told to produce television that would redeem colour's reputation, promote the new service and create a landmark in programming. The BBC had produced two three-part black-and-white series on antiquity entitled *The Glory That Was Greece* (1959) and *The Grandeur That Was Rome* (1960), in which the novelist Sir Compton Mackenzie visited historic sites and shared his 'reflections'. Now it proposed to get Clark to front a similar series on art history, one that would show the new medium's ability to render familiar masterpieces in colour. It would showcase 'all the loveliest things that western civilisation had created since the last two thousand years . . . a ravishing cavalcade of beautiful things'.[1]

But did Clark have any interest in working for the BBC? In 1955 Clark had taken the highly controversial step of accepting the chairmanship of the Independent Television Authority (ITA), the body charged with supervising the UK's first steps in independent television. Leading figures in the Conservative party had been among those who had questioned the BBC's broadcast monopoly, starting with a key white paper in 1952. That Clark, a figure who seemed to epitomise the patrician values of BBC founder John Reith, should prove a class traitor shocked many. Clark had followed up his ITA chairmanship with a career as presenter of more than fifty ITV arts programmes, doing his bit to address concerns that independent television would lead to a race to the bottom in programme quality.

In 1966 his contract with ITV expired. In inviting Clark to lunch, Attenborough wasn't just sounding him out about a new series: he was welcoming him back to the fold. This lunch at Television Centre soon became something of a legend. At some point Attenborough used the word 'civilisation', at which point Clark's imagination took fire, and he mentally began jotting down a tentative episode list:

> David Attenborough invited me to lunch, saying that he would like to discuss a project with me. He wanted to do a series of fifteen films: 'What shall I call it? Say Civilisation.' I don't think he really intended to use the word, but it slipped out. I was munching my smoked salmon rather

apathetically when I heard it, and suddenly there flashed across my mind a way in which the history of European civilisation from the dark ages to 1914 could be made dramatic and visually interesting. I said 'Let me think about it for half an hour.' I seemed to remember someone saying that I need only be chairman of a committee, and someone else that I need not write the programmes, only narrate them; but my mind was occupied and I did not answer. When we came to the coffee I said 'I will do the programmes. I will write and narrate them. I do not need any outside help.' At this moment Huw Wheldon had joined us and gave me full support. His colleagues felt a little uneasy, but there was nothing they could do about it.[2]

Much remained up in the air. Clark's preferred title for the series was 'What Is Civilisation? A Personal View by Kenneth Clark'. But the BBC decided it did not like the word 'civilisation'. Only after extensive discussion of alternatives was Clark able to retain it (albeit not as part of a question) and the subtitle 'a personal view'. Those three words after the colon seem dispensable today, but they played a vital role in softening a title that might otherwise have had the worst of both worlds: long, polysyllabic – yet monolithic and monumental at the same time. They also protected Clark against those who might accuse him of suffering delusions of comprehensiveness.

A lot was riding on the series. The budget of £15,000 per episode (c. £170,000 today) was an unprecedentedly expensive gamble for the time. In so far as the BBC never included salaries or equipment in such budgets, the real cost was even higher. When first broadcast in February 1969 the series met with considerable critical acclaim. There are stories of village church services being rescheduled and of 'Civilisation parties' that met in the homes of those wealthy enough to possess a colour television. Yet in his autobiography Clark wrote of receiving letters from

people of every shade of thought or education . . . from very simple, almost illiterate people, who could not have understood a quarter of my allusions, to . . . cabinet ministers (including Jim Callaghan) and three Cardinals. The most affecting were letters from people who said that they had been on the point of committing suicide, and that my programmes had saved them.[3]

Only 1 in 200 sets or approximately 100,000 households could receive the colour signal, and large areas of the country were in any case out of reach of the new transmitters that had to be built to carry it. Though it was compared at the time by Barry Norman and others to BBC1's costume drama *The Forsyte Saga* (1967–9), the colour bar prevented *Civilisation* having anything like the same viewing figures.[4] According to the BBC's own estimates only around 1 per cent of the UK adult population watched, rising to around 8 per cent when the series was rebroadcast on BBC1 two years later. The tie-in book of the series was published in 1969, however, and extended the series' impact. It sold over a million copies in the United States, and remains in print.

The increase in viewing figures for the 1971 repeat undoubtedly reflects wider access to colour by 1971. But it may also reflect the feedback from *Civilisation* in America, where the series' reception was even warmer than in the UK. *Civilisation* was first screened in the National Gallery of Art, Washington in November 1969. Word of mouth spread its fame such that the gallery was forced to show each episode continuously. Even then, thousands were turned away. The gallery began a film loan scheme under which the series was shown for free at universities, high schools and public libraries across the country. Only then did the fledgeling non-commercial Public Broadcasting Service bow to pressure and take steps to air the series. Sponsorship from the Xerox Corporation enabled PBS to incorporate *Civilisation* into the core programming stream transmitted to all 200-odd public television stations in the United States, from HETV Honolulu to WNET New York.

Starting on 7 October 1970, episodes of *Civilisation* were shown on Sundays, and repeated on Wednesdays. Although other networks claimed a PBS viewership of just 0.1 per cent, *Civilisation*

received widespread newspaper coverage and was a critical success.
PBS's own figures put the average audience at 950,000. Its profile at a
time when federal funding of public television was under attack by the
Nixon administration made *Civilisation* a poster child for 'quality'
television. It was 'an Adult *Sesame Street*', and Clark was its Big Bird.
With a distinctive beak, curious gait and imposing stature, he too was
under threat from the barbarians. Out in the affiliates the series, tie-in
courses and the *Civilisation* book provided opportunities to raise profile
as well as funds from viewer donations, emphasising the message that
public television was paid for, and produced by, 'viewers like you'.
In Washington, *Civilisation* was the tank the Corporation for Public
Broadcasting (which channelled federal funds into the system) needed to
park on the White House lawn.

Actually, they did better: the series was shown inside the White
House. Mrs Nixon and various cabinet members came – the President
stayed away. PBS won the battle with Nixon, thanks in no small part to
Clark. With the exception of the Shakespeare series *An Age of Kings*
(1961) BBC exports to American non-commercial television had been
one-offs before 1970. What with the follow-on successes of *America*
(1972, aired in the US in 1973), *The Ascent of Man* (1973, aired in the
US in 1975) as well as the countless costume dramas shown on
Masterpiece Theatre, PBS began to look like a fully owned-and-operated
subsidiary of the BBC. As the 1979 Carnegie Commission on public
broadcasting noted, 'the effect on American viewers is the impression
that public television prefers actors and commentators with British
accents'.[5]

Civilisation is a landmark series, and as such has threatened to
become something of a cliché to its critics as well as its fans.
To understand it fully we need to understand rather than condemn these
stereotypes, to recognise the role they played in viewers' self-fashioning
as members of a specific generation, class or profession. In my own
interviews and informal conversations with an unrepresentative sample
of people who remember the series, I have found views to be split
between contempt and admiration. Broadly speaking, anyone who can

remember the series does so fondly, unless they work for the BBC or an art museum, in which case they find the subject embarrassing. To this 'professional' audience directly involved in bringing history and art to the public, *Civilisation* is the show they loved to make fun of at university, taking turns to laugh at their friends' impressions of Clark. The idea that there might be something to learn from the series is dismissed out of hand; the series is patronising, orientalist, relentlessly Whiggish, overly didactic and very, very slow.

In an otherwise highly sensitive reading of PBS history, Laurie Ouellette manages a pitch-perfect rendition of this caricature:

> [Clark is] an embodiment of gentility and expertise with his English title, sophisticated vocabulary, classic tweeds, and bowler hat. Stylistically, its slow-moving and staid camera movements, fetishized close-ups, loving pans of great works of art, and dulcet tones of chamber music conveyed an aura of serious contemplation. Clark's summation of extraordinary achievements presents each instant of artistic and intellectual genius as another step in the steady march of progress. His tour of the greatest music, literature, art, architecture, poetry, science, politics, and philosophy places the Western European high society at the undisputed center of 'man's common heritage' . . . [it] moves at the pace of molasses, relies on static shots of Clark pontificating, and requires a dictionary to follow.[6]

9

Another commentator has written that the series 'almost never admits to uncertainty or doubt, to ambivalence or to the existence of competing theories . . . admitting no gaps or problems, no alternatives and no sense of difference'.[7]

Though interpretations are of course bound to differ, at times I will confess to wondering if these critics and I had watched the same series. Clark didn't pontificate, he hedged. A belief in the steady march of progress was ridiculous. Whiggish and Marxist 'competing theories' *were* mentioned. Clark may occasionally present them in a simplistic fashion, but at least he treats them both the same. Clark *never* wore a bowler hat in *Civilisation*. If he affects any headgear, it is the distinctly unaristocratic cloth cap. 'Oh, that dreadful man with the pipe, always droning on . . .' commented the head of education at a national museum when asked how she recalled the series. Clark never smoked a pipe. Even those who remember the series fondly are guilty of making their own caricature, as an optimistic celebratory tour hailing the 'steady march of progress'. John Walker's account of the series in his survey *Arts TV* is typical in claiming that Clark's 'message was fundamentally positive and optimistic'.[8] The historian Richard Weight is a rare exception, noting the discrepancy between the ambivalent message Clark broadcast and the optimistic one so many viewers opted to receive.[9]

Clark himself was frustrated by the tendency of his viewers to miss the point, above all in America, where the gap between his personal convictions and his public persona yawned most. 'If you listen carefully,' he patiently told an audience in Washington, 'you will find there is a good deal more scepticism in those programmes than most people allow

10

Peter Montagnon and Clark

Rodin's *Burghers of Calais*: intimations of doom?

for.'[10] Those who knew Clark best knew he was a pessimist. One of the directors on *Civilisation* put it this way:

> Although he had intimations of doom, he thought he couldn't deal with them. Neither could [his wife] Jane. About both of them there was that feeling that they had seen it all and they didn't quite want to know what came next.[11]

Fifteen minutes into 'The Skin of Our Teeth' (episode 1) the barbarians defeat the classical world. Clark escapes to Ireland. If it wanted to survive 'civilisation would now have to face the Atlantic'. The camera pans over a blasted Irish moor. 'What a hope!'

For good or ill, *Civilisation* has become identified with a pompous, self-congratulatory 'presenter as hero' model. My own experience suggests that within the BBC the series is now seen as a cautionary catalogue of mistakes to be avoided. The 'c-word' itself is shunned by all save Neo-Cons eager to script recent events as yet another episode in 'The Clash of Civilisations'. As we celebrate its fortieth anniversary, it is time we had a fairer, less schematic assessment of the series: to go beyond the caricature of smug reassurance, scholarly hauteur and exclusive aestheticism to consider the series' portrayal of civilisation as fragile, yet open to discussion by everyone.

11

This book begins with a chapter providing background to Attenborough's commission. It places this series within the broader context of Clark's career as well as that of director Michael Gill, and includes close readings of Clark's ITV arts documentaries, Gill's early work and BBC's *Monitor* (1958–65). The second chapter attempts to pin down what Clark meant by 'civilisation', and just how he knew it when he saw it – or heard it, or touched it. I suggest that there is a way of piecing together all thirteen episodes other than as a crescendo, and show the ways in which direction, editing and even the handicaps imposed by technology were harnessed to get the 'shape of civilisation' right. The next two chapters consider the critical and popular reaction to the show, first in the UK and then in the United States. It should not be forgotten that *Civilisation* also met with popular acclaim when it was broadcast in Australia, New Zealand, Canada, Switzerland, Germany, Sweden, Finland, Ireland, Yugoslavia, Holland, Belgium and Bulgaria. Despite the high profile it gave to 'their' history, it proved surprisingly difficult to get it redubbed for French and Italian television. Although *Civilisation* did eventually cross the channel, at the time Clark concluded that the French and Italians were 'too jolly grand' to accept a British series on culture.[12] For reasons of space, this book focuses exclusively on the British and American response. A final chapter considers John Berger's series, *Ways of Seeing* (1970) as well as *America* (1972) and *Ascent of Man* (1973), which followed the *Civilisation* model closely, even as they sought to tweak it. It also considers later series by Robert Hughes, Simon Schama and others.

Justifying *Civilisation*'s 'classic' status is on one level straightforward. The series was the BBC's first authored documentary series to be filmed in colour, and holds the same place in PBS history. It pushed the available 35mm film technology to its limits, including special effects. It spawned many imitators and would-be imitators, to the point that it threatened to become a cliché. But if we try to go any further we encounter only paradox. *Civilisation* is a loving look backwards, commissioned to show off the new wonders of high-definition colour broadcasting. It is a declaration of confidence in mankind's potential, presented by a pessimist. A celebration of continuity, at a time of dislocation. A show next to nobody watched, but which everybody remembers. If we can resolve these paradoxes, then perhaps we can learn something from *Civilisation*.

2 Mating Pandas

My fear is that my kind of programme is rather old-fashioned – as is my approach to the subject. If one tried to hot it up there would be a discord or conflict. Of course my style, and content, might be a bit too square and stuffy – in that case get John Berger, who seems to have worked successfully with Michael Gill. I think this would really be more in keeping with current BBC policy.[13]

Clark to Humphrey Burton

That Television Centre lunch with Attenborough and Wheldon had certainly lit a spark in Clark's mind. Attenborough's apparently accidental reference to 'civilisation' immediately set him thinking about how a series might be structured around it. A word casually dropped in conversation would become the capstone of a television landmark. Given the nature of the industry and the profile of the parties concerned, it is inevitable that the lunch quickly became the first of a series of moments that passed into myth. The real story behind the series is more complex, punctuated by hesitation, misunderstanding and compromise. Although the BBC had seemed his natural home during the war, sixteen years spent in independent television had left Clark with an outsider's view of the corporation. The BBC itself had moved on since the days of Lord Reith. The 1960s saw BBC television grow at an unprecedented pace, admitting a new generation who saw the medium as one of exploration and experimentation rather than exposition. To this generation Clark seemed remote. As Michael Gill later observed,

David Attenborough

Clark seemed 'glittering, self-possessed, armed with precise certainties'. He 'seemed to epitomise attitudes the opposite of those of my friends and myself'.[14]

The BBC's Head of Arts, Humphrey Burton likened the challenge of bringing Gill and Clark together with that of mating pandas. The simile says as much about the zoo-keepers at Television Centre as it does about the pandas. But a contrast in background, in attitudes and approach to the medium of television there certainly was, a contrast which almost defeated the project. In another letter to Burton, Clark explained his reluctance to comply with the directors' three main criticisms of his first script.

> First [Gill] thought that we must find a title for the series which does not include the word 'civilisation'. Secondly, he thought I should write with greater warmth and, thirdly, that I should make the scripts even more personal than they are already.[15]

Gill's memoirs have the directors teaching Clark to write and present in a new way – a line Clark's autobiography seems to support. Part of this re-education involved encouraging Clark to expose more of his own character. Although he met several of the directors' demands, Clark successfully defended 'civilisation'. This concept is discussed in the next chapter. But before considering the series in detail we first need to understand the triangular relationship between Clark, the directors and the corporation that brought them together.

Trahison de Clark

Though there is no denying its large size, the Clark fortune was new by the standards of pre-war society. Wealth earned in his grandfather's Paisley thread works was gambled by his father on the tables of Monte Carlo. Clark's youth was divided between hotels on the Riviera and a characterless house in Suffolk. His parents were not particularly affectionate, though there was nothing unusual for the time in that. His father encouraged his son's interest in art. Educated at Winchester and Oxford, Clark served his apprenticeship in Italy with the great art expert Bernard Berenson. A keepership of western art at the Ashmolean Museum in Oxford was followed by the directorship of the National Gallery. He married Jane in 1927, and the pair moved in one of the most glamorous circles of interwar society: the Duff Coopers, Cecil Beaton, Sibyl Colefax. Boredom was their greatest fear. Years later Clark could behave with remarkable rudeness to people he considered dull.

The war brought this golden age (which Clark dubbed 'the Clark Boom' in his memoirs) to a sudden end. There is little sense that Clark mourned its passing. He had already taken his first steps in arts television, presenting *The Genius of the Florentines* in December 1937, just thirteen months after BBC's first television broadcast. Described as 'a showing of pictures with a commentary', this was one of a strand entitled *Artists and Their Work*, broadcast from Alexandra Palace.[16]

Clark by
Howard Coster

17

Although he conceded the poor quality of the images received, Clark thought 'the process would be of immense importance in popularising the [National] Gallery if ever it attained the necessary degree of proficiency'.[17] Two years later his expertise in 'pictures' led to him being assigned to the film department of the Ministry of Information, where he produced films such as *Mrs Grant Goes to the Door* (1939), a public-information short advising people how they should behave after a German invasion. Although he conceded that film was an infant medium, Clark's viewing of wartime features such as *Mr Smith Goes to Washington* (1939) and *Let George Do It!* (1940) had left him pessimistic. Feature-length films inevitably showed 'the hopelessness of man's struggle against natural forces'. Film, he concluded, 'tends to be a destructive rather than a constructive agent'.[18]

Clark felt his work on the War Artists Advisory Council to be far more important. Thanks to his efforts a state that was highly sceptical of government patronage commissioned artists such as John Piper, Graham Sutherland and Henry Moore to produce work recording an imperilled landscape and heritage. The results were sent on tour by the Council for the Encouragement of Music and the Arts (CEMA, the predecessor of the Arts Council) and celebrated in films such as Jill Craigie's *Out of Chaos* (1944). Such 'elemental and timeless' work would, it was hinted, be much more widely admired in the new world that waited at the end of the war, a world shorn of highbrows. Although Clark would later serve as chairman of the Arts Council (1953–60), there is little to suggest that he shared such hopes, that he believed 'the bright new world stuff in the weekly papers'.[19] Utopian visions of a democratic culture were nonetheless necessary to secure government funds.

These visions were also rather embarrassing, something that had – like the Arts Council bureaucracy itself – to be tolerated as the price of protecting a few artists from penury. After all, to quote the first film ever sponsored by the Arts Council, *Artists Must Live*. The documentary 'encounters' produced by John Read in the 1950s maintained this focus on artists, rather than art. They placed a strong emphasis on craft and process, following the steps by which Piper created an aquatint, for example. And their subjects were the same cohort of artists that Clark had sponsored during the war: Piper, Sutherland and Moore. Clark personally revelled in their company. It was a refreshing contrast to the monied elite of the 1930s, as well as to the National Gallery curators who had never considered him a real scholar. Even so, Clark's patrician reserve remained.

So did the fear of being bored. In 1954 Clark became first chairman of the Independent Television Authority (ITA). As Bernard Sendall has noted, at the time 'nobody quite knew what to make of the appointment of Clark'.[20] He didn't own a television himself. As for the BBC, at the time it considered Clark to be 'essentially a BBC man, rather than an ITV man'.[21] In the mid-1950s it seemed that the mandarins of

18

the 'intellectual aristocracy' had never had it so good. Clark was a traitor, booed in the dining room of the Athenaeum, his club. Clark later justified the act to himself as another case of trying to salvage what he could before the deluge came and swept everything away. More could be done to hold back the 'avalanche of vulgarity' from inside.

With hindsight his insistence that holders of ITV franchises club together to fund a single Independent Television News (ITN) was inspired. Any explanation of Clark's 'betrayal' would be incomplete, however, without noting the extent to which Clark fell under the spell of charismatic commercial television executives, Lew Grade above all. Born Louis Winogradsky in the Ukraine, as a child Grade had toured British music halls in the 1920s before becoming London's top theatrical agent. Thanks to financial backing from Warburgs he was able to move into television, forming the Independent Television Company, which took a 50 per cent stake in Associated Television (ATV), one of the firms licensed by the ITA. ATV went on to create *Crossroads* (1964–88), and launched the careers of Roger Moore (*The Saint*, 1962–9, *The Persuaders*, 1971–2) and Patrick McGoohan (*Danger Man*, 1964–6, *The Prisoner*, 1967–8).

19

After a disastrous first couple of years in which several television companies almost went to the wall, by early 1957 an independent television franchise had become (in Roy Thomson's famous phrase) 'a licence to print money'. ITV whittled the BBC's share of television viewers down to 51 per cent. Meanwhile the number of television sets increased from 5 million in 1956 to 13 million in 1964. As far as Clark was concerned, ITV may have been vulgar, but after the Arts Council its dynamism and success made it a fizzy, if slightly guilty pleasure – like the Coca-Cola that Clark used to sneak downstairs and drink surreptitiously in the middle of the night.[22] Clark's admiration for Grade was reciprocated, and when Clark's ITA chairmanship ended Grade pounced, signing Clark up to a ten-year contract. The BBC would have to wait until 1966 to reclaim 'their' man.

Although they are almost totally forgotten today, Clark made forty-eight programmes for ATV. By 1963 it was possible for the

'I don't know how
this is going to
come off'

Observer's critic to praise Clark's performance in terms that prefigure
the response to *Civilisation*:

> He has long since got over the diffidence and stiffness of his early
> appearances, but the first of his new Monday series *Discovering Japanese
> Art* seemed to touch a new peak in the technique of the art lecture.
> Manner and matter were beautifully blended in an unselfconscious
> assumption of equality with the audience. This was a genuine feat of
> communication. Sir Kenneth was helped, of course, by the convenient
> autobiographical travelogueish framework.[23]

Though they often went out half an hour later than the BBC's arts
magazine *Monitor*, at 10:30pm, Clark's ATV shows garnered ratings
more than three times higher.[24]

   The pilot of his first art series in 1958 was, however, carefully
chaperoned by ATV, the network that would broadcast most of his ITV
output. The title, *Is Art Necessary?* posed a question that one suspects
many ITV executives had already been asking themselves privately.
The episode opens, not with Kenneth, but with William Clark (no
relation), whose headmasterly introduction is delivered with all the
robotic charm of a public-health warning:

20

Good evening. We are starting now on a new and exciting exploration. We're going to explore the feelings and the ideas that lie behind our attitude towards beautiful things, and the leader of our exploration is Sir Kenneth Clark, who might really be called one of the world's greatest experts on art. But there's one thing I want to make quite clear. This is *not* a programme written by experts on art for experts on art *at all*. We've planned to deal with ordinary, simple things that one finds in the home. Not the sort of thing you'd expect to find salted away in gloomy and cold art galleries, but ordinary, everyday things, cats and dogs . . . .

The rest of the episode consists of studio discussion of animal aesthetics between the two Clarks and a series of rare horse and sheep breeders, illustrated by film of agricultural fairs.

Later episodes had Clark consider 'What is good taste?' by comparing studio mock-ups of 'good' and 'bad' living rooms – the 'bad' had antimacassars, three flying ducks on the wall and (revealingly) a

21

ATV arts programming: on a tight leash?

television. Other episodes considered public sculpture, portraiture and value. Short interviews featured occasionally, and studio guests included artists and critics. Clark was happy to have John Berger on to discuss Picasso's *Guernica*. When Clark argued that the distortions of modern art were illegible to the majority Berger responded with a beer poster featuring a similar, yet immediately legible, distortion of the human form. Consumer culture, something Clark always saw as 'trivial', was now (Berger proposed) the only one able to provide that 'unity of ideals and values' that made communication possible. The encounter is fascinating to watch today, quite apart from its anticipation of points Berger would make in *Ways of Seeing*. Looking back almost twenty years later, Clark interpreted his director's introduction of these 'more experienced performers' as an attempt to 'swamp me'. 'The result was a shambles. It must have been one of the worst programmes ever put on, and was generally recognised as such.'[25] In fact, the series had its admirers. Writing eight years later in 1966, Norman Swallow claimed

22

John Berger and Clark

that it was still 'probably the most effective concentrated attempt by television to treat art seriously and at the same time hold as large an audience as possible'.[26]

Clark went on to write and present *Five Revolutionary Painters* (1959), which he considered 'my first real success'.[27] He was being watched in 1.6 million homes, representing at least 2.5 million viewers. This represented a significantly larger audience than the 750,000 for Oxford history don A. J. P. Taylor's 1958 lectures.[28] Later series included *The Art of Landscape Painting* (1961), *Discovering Japanese Art* (1963), *Great Temples of the World* (1964), *Rediscovering the Image* (1965), *Royal Palaces* (1966) as well as other programmes. Many of Clark's ATV programmes are now lost. Before the advent of video tape in 1959 a lot of television went out live, including drama, and was unrecorded. Clark later concluded that without this experience of 'the old days of live transmission . . . I might not have been able to do the filmed sequences of *Civilisation* with as much vivacity'.[29]

After 1959 video tape was expensive, and many programmes were wiped so that the tape could be reused. Production values were low, even on those programmes filmed on 16mm. A forty-five-minute episode would be rehearsed and filmed over two afternoons in a studio. In the five years after *Is Art Necessary?*, these studios could be spartan affairs, with a single stool that Clark seemed reluctant to leave. Illustration was provided either by cutting away to stills or by the use of large unframed reproductions in the studio. Although he had a script at hand, just out of vision, these programmes felt unscripted, and often struggled to maintain momentum under the weight of all the qualifications, hypotheticals and open-ended questions with which the presenter loaded his subject. Illustrations came at a fast pace, so fast that Clark often struggled to come to a satisfying conclusion at the end.

Things improved somewhat after 1962 as a result of ITV's attempts to raise its arts profile after a poor performance before the Pilkington Committee on Broadcasting (1960–2). Led by the industrialist Sir Harry Pilkington, the Pilkington Report heavily criticised ITV as well as the ITA for lowering standards. Thanks in part to the machinations of its Director-General, Sir Hugh Carleton Greene, the BBC had by contrast been highly praised, with the report urging government to grant the BBC a second television channel. Even before the report appeared ITV began to fight back. Arts magazine *Tempo* was started in 1961 as a 'swinging *Monitor*', for example, though all arts shows were still kept well away from primetime. Clark's programmes left the 'still and stool' behind, in a somewhat half-hearted attempt to move towards travelogue. Stills of Clark visiting buildings were taken and padded out with footage that had been bought in. The rest was done with studio fakery: back projection, an ersatz rock or two on which Clark could sit while pretending to speak to camera from Karnak. The illusion was exploited to provide the clear breaks that the script failed to furnish. Clark abruptly interrupts his line of thought because he claims he is tired, or because it is time for lunch. In the case of Karnak a hot climate was suggested by giving Clark a white golfing cap to wear. The result looked 'hokey as hell'.[30]

As a presenter Clark always seemed doubtful of the medium's ability to get any meaningful thoughts through to the viewer. Similar concerns would make Berger intense and passionate in *Ways of Seeing*. In Clark's case it had the opposite effect. Profound doubt unleashed a playfulness that could seem blithely arrogant. It takes a daring presenter to open a new series with the line 'I don't know how this is going to come off', the line which begins *Five Revolutionary Painters*. When Clark observed in *Great Temples*, 'I am not an Egyptologist. I am a learner, so I hope I don't make too many howlers', there was a sense in which he was thumbing his nose at the experts. Helped by the travelogue format, Clark forged an easy-going compact with the viewer. Let the scholars cavil, he seems to say, we know what is really interesting and important.

Clark had also realised the important distinction between television 'talks' and television lectures. As he observed in his 1966 Granada Lecture:

> It is a curious fact that millions of people will watch a man talking who would not listen to his disembodied voice. That is because he is talking to

them personally. He must not lecture and he must not orate. He must use
the short sentences and staccato rhythms of conversation.[31]

In this Clark was making a clear distinction between his type of 'talk'
and the lectures of the sort Taylor had been giving on ATV since 1957.
At times overly provocative, at others sulky or simply rude, Taylor's
behaviour on air had got him pushed off BBC television and radio.
He went on to become an active campaigner for independent television.

The programmes played to Taylor's gladiatorial strengths.
Taylor was supposedly responding to a 'challenge'. As the announcer
put it at the start, 'ATV presents an experiment. Can a brilliant historian
talking about a fascinating subject hold the attention of a television
audience of millions for half an hour? That is the question, and the
answer lies with YOU.' Taylor then marched, head down, onto a
blacked-out stage, nodded stiffly at the audience, bid them 'Good
evening', and began. Taylor upped the ante by lecturing without notes,
and maintained interest by focusing on individual life stories and violent
events. Initially a great success, too much of the appeal lay in the
novelty. Once Taylor proved he could do it, delivering perfectly timed
lectures time and again like clockwork, the format began to seem tired.
Taylor's appearances declined after 1962, even as his producer added a
few props and introductory visuals.[32] In 1964 BBC2 launched a new
type of television history, in which an international team of scholars,
eyewitness interviews and mountains of archival footage were deployed
without a presenter. Twenty-six episodes long, *The Great War* was
narrated by Sir Michael Redgrave, with other actors reading quotations
from contemporary observers of the conflict. By 1966 Clark was
speaking the television lecture's epitaph. For the most part his Granada
Lecture was pessimistic about the future of television and the medium's
ability to deliver quality programming.

Clark's views reflected his experience at the ITA ten years
before. Like many an honest broker, as ITA chairman, Clark had made
himself unpopular with both sides, with government and the ITV
franchise-holders. Between 1956 and 1958 he had pushed the Treasury

25

and Paymaster General (the minister responsible for broadcasting) to make good on a promise they had made back in 1954 to provide £750,000 for the ITA to spend on commissioning news, education and 'minority' programming. It was important, he believed, for the ITA to have such a fund, partly to make the authority appear less of a lightweight in negotiations with television companies, and partly to enable it to maintain certain standards. After much wrangling the Paymaster General offered a derisory £100,000, which the ITV companies were delighted to refuse. They could now forget their obligations to education and 'minority' programming under the original Act *and* blame the government for it. Clark was left in the middle. He prepared to make what would have been a very public resignation in late 1956, but backed down.[33]

Clark did not remain quiet for long. As Bernard Sendall has noted in his history of independent television in Britain, Clark was 'a kind of Jekyll and Hyde in television affairs'. In 1955 Clark may have seemed a 'traitor' to the BBC, but his Granada Lecture and his evidence to the Pilkington Committee could seem equally disloyal to his new colleagues in ITV. To quote Sendall,

> There was the Jekyll who launched ITV and saw it through its initial difficulties with brilliant success. He was tolerant and considerate and displayed infinite resource. He withdrew [from the ITA] after three years, to the universal disappointment of his ITV friends. He states [in his autobiography] that he was not asked to stay on and hated leaving. There was the Hyde who subsequently presented disparaging and destructive evidence to the Pilkington Committee. He was an aesthete and an intellectual, and yet in his dealings with the whole range of Independent Television from the tycoons to the bureaucrats he showed no hint of condescension.[34]

In his evidence to Sir Harry Pilkington, Clark had indeed warned that 'more control will be needed to prevent a Gadarene descent' at ITV.

In 1966 Clark produced his last ITV programme, which was also his first colour film. *Royal Palaces* was an ITV/BBC co-production filmed on 35mm stock for broadcast on Christmas Day. As *Variety* noted, Clark's 'urbane narration . . . wasn't scared of some sly digs at certain manifestations of the royal taste'.[35] The Royal Family were unamused. Though the series was a showcase for what colour could do in the best hands, it was clear even before Clark's Pilkington evidence that ITV would never devote sufficient resources for a series. *Discovering Japanese Art* had been only four episodes, *Temples* stopped after two, *Royal Palaces* was a one-off.

Happily, Clark's contract expired a few days after *Royal Palaces* was broadcast. And this time it was the BBC that was ready to pounce.

Indulgent Mandarins

Among the Clark Papers at the Tate is a small red notebook. Several pages in, after scribbled notes on Rembrandt and Egyptian monuments is the first *Civilisation* episode list he wrote. Fourteen in all, one more than the BBC schedulers would eventually allow. Clark has gone back and crossed out number 7 (on Spain) at a later date – a decision which would haunt him later. Over the following pages he fleshes out his ideas in his tiny handwriting. Before doing that, however, Clark made a second list, entitled 'Warn BBC':

> Not marxist,
> not a history of economics, nor of political ideals.
> Of ethics only in rather a specialised sense –
> religion will play a bigger part than economics.

As for the choice of director, he went on, 'anyone worth employing will want to do the whole thing in his own way'.[36] Thirty years on from his first appearance on the BBC, Clark clearly feared that if he accepted Wheldon's offer he would have to put up with Marxist prima donnas with political issues. And at sixty-three he was no longer up for that. The BBC should ask John Berger instead.

When he referred in the letter quoted at the start of this chapter to 'current BBC policy', Clark was probably thinking of *Monitor*, a weekly arts magazine which began in 1958, the same year as Clark's *Is Art Necessary?*, and ran until 1965. Under the watchful eye of Wheldon, the 'earnest headmaster', *Monitor* had provided a sandbox in which a

Allan Tyrer, Ken Russell and Huw Wheldon

series of young directors had experimented, many of whom went on to become distinguished feature-film directors. Chief among these was Ken Russell. His 1962 Elgar biopic broke the BBC's unwritten rule which forbade dramatisation in documentaries, on the grounds that it was tantamount to misrepresentation. The costumed actors remained silent, however, a series of vignettes that jarred somewhat against the earnestly informative narrator and archive footage, duped by a trainee editor, Roger Crittenden, who later cut *Civilisation*. As Gill later observed:

> Taking a few of the more exotic known facts about his subject, Russell embroiders and enlarges them into the form of lyrical and erotic dreams . . . . He attempts to give visible form to those secret obsessions which gave the artist his creative energy. This must be highly subjective, and often Russell appears to be recording the fantasies which the artist has given *him*, rather than saying anything profound about the artist himself . . . what Russell is doing is actually the contemporary equivalent of those 19th-century

Elgar

paintings in which Dante gazes longingly at the distant Beatrice, or the young Raleigh looks out over the windswept Atlantic.[37]

Elgar continues to enjoy a high reputation, preferred to later Russell documentaries in which the actors did speak, such as *Always on Sunday* (1965) on the painter Henri Rousseau, *The Debussy Film* (1965) and *Dante's Inferno* (1967) on Rossetti.

The shorter mini-documentaries presented to camera by John Berger and others arguably fitted *Monitor*'s magazine format better. The best of these emerged – as Michael Gill's *Why Leger?* (1958) did – from a dialogue between director and presenter. Those which simply assumed that all artists had something profound to say about their own work could drag, as Russell's *Pop Goes the Easel* (1962) definitely did. Peter Blake, Derek Boshier, Peter Phillips and Pauline Boty took turns at being their own auteur, quoting music, Westerns and the celebrity interview. Such bricolage could have been genuinely creative. The film begins with a sceptical Wheldon introducing them. Headmaster to his fingertips, he tells us what each artist's father does for a living. The show ends with all four back in the studio and behaving themselves, heads down, quietly getting on with their work. While such artists were occasionally allowed to play with the lights or even hold on to the wheel for a second, there was no doubt that Wheldon kept his feet on *Monitor*'s pedals.

Although Ann Turner and Allan Tyrer were part of the *Monitor* team, apart from the odd segment Gill was not. The son of a bank manager, Gill's childhood in rural Kent was lonely but happy. Frequent bouts of bovine tuberculosis confined him to a spinal chair for several years, and later relapses repeatedly interrupted his career, first in the Air Force Reserve, then as a philosophy student at Edinburgh and finally as a director. Gill started at the BBC in 1954, and initially specialised in educational films, where he worked closely with Peter Montagnon, the critic David Sylvester and John Berger. Gill also produced documentaries on individual artists, including Alberto Giacometti and Francis Bacon, the latter incorporating jagged cross-cutting techniques evoking the artist's manner.

31

Gill's forty-four-minute documentary *Francis Bacon: Fragments of a Portrait* was broadcast on BBC1 in September 1966. Sylvester was credited as programme advisor, and the film is built around an interview between him and the artist in his studio. It was a development of the 'encounter' documentary, a format originally developed by John Read. Like Read's film of John Piper (1955) it dwells on the clutter of the studio, and suggests the possibility of observing the artist at work. Experience of attempting to film Giacometti had sensitised Gill to the difficulties surrounding this voyeuristic concept, which was, he concluded, a conceit. In *Fragments* it has become a tease. The programme ends with Bacon walking up to a blank canvas, preparing to paint his first stroke – which we never get to see.

Instead *Fragments* endeavours to recreate the world of Bacon's portraits through a series of sequences combining stills and slow-motion photography overlaid with a dissonant original score composed by Edwin Astley, who later composed music for *Civilisation*. These suggest

From *Bacon* . . .

a mood of menace, particularly by means of cross-cutting between slow-motion film of Bacon's own mouth and details of screaming mouths taken from his paintings. Another sequence follows a discussion of Bacon's interest in meat, and intercuts film of abattoirs and a supermarket meat counter. The results make Sylvester's interview and somnolent voice-over appear ponderous. The interview is unsuccessful, largely because Sylvester is asking the wrong questions, constantly returning to an undifferentiated public's shock at Bacon's output. Film of the pair going on a run to the shops smacks of a desperate attempt to pass the time. Gill's later comments on the challenges associated with such 'artist-at-work' documentaries seem to speak directly to *Fragments*:

> There is an element of imposture in most fly's eye views of an artist's studio. Art is a private business, and film demands a compression of time and a dramatic development with a beginning, middle and end that few artists can achieve in the relatively circumscribed time that they are going

to allow their studio to be invaded, lit and photographed . . . . Ideally it's the moment when Michelangelo paints in the fingers of God and Adam that the film director wants to record. And when he can't get this he falls back on those endless shots of Michelangelo climbing up the scaffolding, strolling round the square of St Peter's, buying his spaghetti, which fill up so many art films of the last ten years. These insights are usually accompanied by a breathy, pretentious and irrelevant commentary, recorded elsewhere on tape by the artist himself, on the theme of his secret aspirations, or what he would like the world to believe they were.

Such was the 'hothouse pressure of television', Gill continued, that the 'artist-at-work' film 'has gone straight from Primitive to Mannerist in under one decade'.[38]

Unlike Montagnon, Gill was tempted by features. In 1963 he produced a fifteen-minute short starring Juliet Harmer and narrated by Peter Ustinov that went on to represent Britain at Cannes. Written by his

33

. . . to *Peaches*

then wife, the actress Yvonne Gilan and funded by an improbably small grant from the BFI's Experimental Film Fund, *The Peaches* was a fairy-tale for adults: fun, sexy and slightly gnomic. When it came to choosing something to show Clark in those early panda days Gill elected not to serve *Bacon* or *Peaches*. It would be wrong to call Gill a disappointed features director, however. As Crittenden later observed 'He was always looking for an area that was somewhere between documentary and fiction, somewhere between narrative and something more expressive. It was always going to be difficult to find a home for that kind of work.'[39]

Gill later developed plans for a film, *The Quest*, which would have woven together the medieval concept of chivalry and the story of a man's discovery of a woman's body. The project never came off, though Gill would later write a book entitled *The Image of the Body: Aspects of the Nude* (1989).

He was not entirely immune from the tendency to exploit the 'swinging' scene for formulaic encounter documentaries. At the time he was asked to direct *Civilisation* Gill was struggling to contain the fallout he expected from a film, *Three Swings on a Pendulum* (1966), which followed Lewis Nkosi, Robert Hughes and Olivier Todd as they navigated swinging London. A Nigerian, an Australian and a Frenchman went into several bars. A formula in search of a punchline, the show failed in much the same way the 'edgier' *Monitor*s did. As far as Burton was concerned, however, Gill had proved himself in his earlier one-offs. Gill was, he reassured Clark, 'gifted and anything but a whizz-kid or a Marxist!'[40]

The Glory and the Grandeur

Also present at the Television Centre lunch had been Head of Music and Arts Stephen Hearst, who in 1959–60 had produced two series that also involved inviting a mature broadcast personality to share personal reflections on great civilisations: *The Glory That Was Greece* (1959) and *The Grandeur That Was Rome* (1960), which were subtitled

'Reflections by Sir Compton Mackenzie'. As far as the BBC was concerned these series and not *Monitor* were the closest thing to a precedent for the new project. *Glory*'s three episodes each focused on a great war between good and evil: between Athenian democracy and Spartan militarism ('The Age of Civil War'), between the united Greeks and the Persian empire ('The Age of Victory') and – a foray into mythology – Theseus and the Minotaur ('The Age of Minos'). *Grandeur* adopted a broader approach, starting with the garrison and transport infrastructure that held the Roman empire together ('Skeleton of an Empire'), then considering Christianity's triumph over its rival cults ('Gods and Men') and finishing with a look at the engineering and architecture of aqueducts and other public buildings ('Roman Art and Architecture').

In each forty-minute episode Mackenzie goes on a journey. Short clips show the spry seventy-six-year-old in a series of locations, dressed in a light-coloured three-piece suit with a bow tie and a cane.

Compton Mackenzie

Mackenzie's measured phrases are often used in voice-over, laid over
Charles de Jaeger's film of the Greek landscape, a beach and a boat.
In 'The Age of Victory' there is an attempt to show the battlefield as the
Greeks and Persians would have seen it. The camera slinks up and
'hides' behind a bush, then branches are pulled away to show the field
where the battle was fought. Later Eucles' famous run from Marathon
to Athens is recreated in a long sequence in which the camera 'runs'
through trees and along a pavement. Background music (generic
'classical', with some sallies towards the 'difficult', atonal end of the
spectrum) suggests certain moods: the clash of battle, suspense, anxiety,
etc. When speaking in vision, Mackenzie stands still, usually shown at
full length against back-projection of the location, into which tourists
and on one occasion a bus aimlessly drift. Filmed in Ealing Studios,
these attempts to suggest that Mackenzie is in fact on location appear
ludicrous today. Even for the time, they are overly ambitious and clunky.
At one point Mackenzie tells us of how he 'gazes with reverence' on the
memorial mound at Marathon, and dutifully does so – gazing straight
ahead when the memorial is behind him. Mackenzie pauses (with
deliberate comic effect) in mock irritation when the wayward bus
(a sound effect is laid over the silent location film) 'interrupts' him.
Stills from vases and coins are used to 'animate' blow-by-blow accounts
of battles.

At the time of filming Mackenzie (1883–1972) was a good ten
years older than Clark would be when he came to film *Civilisation*.
Born into a family of actors and theatre managers, educated at St Paul's
and Oxford, Mackenzie had enjoyed considerable literary acclaim for
his early novels, whose promise Henry James and other Edwardian
titans had acknowledged. After the Great War, however, his star seemed
to wane. He withdrew to a series of island retreats (first in Greece, then
Scotland) and built up a very different reputation writing comedies
(*Whisky Galore!*, 1947), histories, biographies and travel books that
celebrated the resilience of the little nation, romantically struggling
against the imperial oppressor. A renowned raconteur and mimic,
Mackenzie had been quick to spot the potential of broadcasting,

establishing *Vox*, the first magazine devoted to the infant industry, in 1926. By the late 1950s he was a celebrity, an outspoken if windy advocate for a series of doomed if romantic causes, author of over 100 books, most of them produced hastily to remedy another financial crisis.

BBC executives like Hearst were not the only ones to see Mackenzie's series as a model. Gill did so, too, and there are several important areas in which these series prepared the ground. They took the presenter outside the studio, and were constructed as journeys 'back' to places that held personal as well as historical significance for 'our guide'. Mackenzie had served in the Dardanelles in 1915, and subsequently ran army intelligence in the Aegean theatre. His shows are 'reflections' on freedom, government and politics illustrated with traditional chronologies of battles and treaties, rather than the other way around. 'Age of Victory' ends with Mackenzie reading an extended passage from one of his own books, in which he muses on how the Greeks' victory ensured the triumph of a progressive, if violent, civilisation over a contented yet static empire. 'The Hellenic victory secured to the world a certainty of continuous war for centuries, by affirming the value of national freedom and individual liberty at whatever the cost to material progress.'

In the end *The Glory That Was Greece* is a failure. Sequences that rapidly cut between stills were intended, by their flitting restlessness, to give something of the mood of a battle. But they represent an abuse of the artefacts: details from a Greek vase are shown once, then reversed and shown again, a detail of a Persian soldier's head from a bas-relief is also shown twice – the second time turned ninety degrees, 'lying down' to represent the enemy dead. Unlabelled charts are shown, then pulled away before we can grasp their content. Meanwhile we never learn what a Greek trireme actually looked like. For all his well-deserved reputation as a master of dialogue and radio commentary, on screen Mackenzie is poor. This is not because of his somewhat advanced age. The raconteur simply suborns the presenter. Mackenzie rarely looks at the camera, gazing instead into the middle distance, tugging at his chin and inserting extempore asides that confuse rather than elucidate. Impressive in scripted voice-over, when in vision Mackenzie's delivery is that of a club bore: avuncular yet abstracted, wallowing in nostalgia, always on the edge of losing the thread.[41] When he does look at us it is with a pained expression, as if embarrassed at having forgotten our names.

The series contained several lessons for Clark and Gill. Clark, for example, would quickly recognise that 'every word must be scripted', right down to the tangents and the asides, and that his words had to follow the rhythms of conversation, where insights appear and are immediately shared, rather than anecdote, where a story is rehearsed and recounted, with pauses for an occasional ornament.[42] *Glory's* grandiloquent title, softened by the subtitle ('Reflections by . . .') also set the stage for a certain amount of wrangling over the title of Clark's series, one known as the 'Western Civilisation Project' within the BBC. Countless alternatives were proposed: *One Thousand Years: Reflections on Art and Western Civilisation, The Art of Civilisation, Roads to Civilisation, Mirror Up to Nature* and the positively dire *Civilisation and Its Contents.* The subtitle 'A Personal View' was a constant in such lists. Attenborough and Burton insisted on having the word 'art', which Clark thought would put the British public off. Gill and Montagnon didn't want the word 'civilisation' at all. Such debates simmered, but the project could go forward.

Although Clark had appointed historian John Hale and art historian Ernst Gombrich as his official academic advisors on the series, in practice he hardly consulted them. If any outside advisors had an impact, it was Clark's own children. Two of them, Colette and Colin, played a crucial role in pre-production. An Oxford history graduate, at the point when Clark finished his first script, Colette had just given birth to a son. Her father visited her in hospital, bringing the script (for episode 4) with him. Though Clark himself 'did not find it at all bad', when he read it aloud Colette told him he was presuming far too much knowledge on the part of the viewer, and that it sounded like a lecture.[43] Colin had followed his father into television, and in 1966 was producing a film about documentary which featured Gill as one of the masters of the genre. Whether prompted by Gill or on his own initiative Colin echoed Colette's critique, advising his father to drop his original refusal to go on location.

Relations between Clark and Gill were nonetheless frosty as the project got under way. With all his ATV experience under his belt, Clark was anything but a television amateur happy to receive direction. A veteran committee chair, he was used to taking charge of others rather than collaborating as an equal. One of the more interesting aspects of the making of *Civilisation* is the story of how the initial conflicts of vision between Clark and the directors bore fruit. Rather than retreating behind red lines, struggling to get as much of 'their' input into the final cut as possible, all parties drew the best out of each other, and out of Clark in particular. Though he claimed to be set in his ways, in fact Clark proved as willing to learn as to teach.

For Clark the many long journeys made in the course of filming *Civilisation* represented something of an autobiographical tour, full of emotional reunions with artefacts, buildings and sites he had visited in happier days before the war. Having his troubled wife Jane along only added to their poignancy. Reason enough, one might have thought, for *Civilisation* to wallow in nostalgia. But something happened on location. In the presence of these objects and revisiting these places Clark was rejuvenated. The crew soon established an easy-going rapport with him, learning from Clark about art, history and literature on and off camera. They served him as a trial audience, their questions highlighting areas that had not been adequately explained. To those who knew Clark in London, the image of him wandering off on long walks with Bill Paget, a 'mere' grip whose main passion in life was golf would have seemed strange.

Gill had no prior experience of the technical challenges of filming old buildings with low-speed 35mm colour film. Fortunately he was able draw on the highly talented team that had produced Anthony de Lotbiniere's 1966 ITV/BBC co-production *Royal Palaces*, which had been presented by Clark and filmed on 35mm colour stock. This was led by lighting cameraman Arthur Adolf Englander, whose career stretched

39

back to 1931, and included work on features at Stoll, Gaumont British, Pinewood and Warner Bros. Englander made secret instructional films in World War II, at which point the Adolf had to go, being replaced first by 'Barrel', then 'Tubby'. Englander joined the BBC in 1952 and filmed the corporation's first colour production, a documentary on the reconstruction of Coventry Cathedral. He would literally write the book on *Filming for Television* (1976). He was assisted by cameraman Ken MacMillan. MacMillan had gained experience of colour filming in west Africa before joining the BBC aged twenty-one, and worked on top BBC dramas of the 1960s, including *Maigret* (1960–3) and *Z Cars* (1962–78). He clearly impressed Clark, who described him as 'an artist, silent, withdrawn and independent . . . when I saw him taking a position different from that suggested by the director, I would give him a wink and a nod of agreement'.[44]

On location in *Royal Palaces*

Together MacMillan and Englander developed new filming methods to allow large, relatively dark historic interiors to be captured on Eastmancolor 5427 stock, which at that point had a very low sensitivity: just 25 ASA in daylight, 50 in tungsten light; 500 ASA film is readily available today. Camera gearboxes were modified to permit the film to run past the lens at reduced speed. *Civilisation* would see such undercranking taken down to an unprecedentedly slow four frames per second. Clark could never appear in undercranked tracking shots. This restricted the directors' ability to have Clark speak to camera inside buildings, except in corners that could be adequately lit using the lamps they had brought with them. This did not stop the crew from achieving some memorable interior shots, starting with the tracking shot inside the Vatican at the end of 'Grandeur and Obedience'. Clark delivers the line, 'I wonder if any thought that has helped forward the human spirit has been conceived or written down in an enormous room,' and walks out of a door in front of us. The camera smoothly retreats, and retreats, and

41

The Austin Dolly

retreats, well past the point at which the viewer expects the camera to reach the opposite wall.

The equipment that the crew took on the road was the best the BBC could provide: two Arriflex 2A cameras (one a handheld), a motorised 5:1 zoom lens, two dollies, 200-volt lights and plenty of track. And, crucially, an Autocue. In studio or out, Autocues were a novelty. The script was typed on an enormous typewriter and then fed into a box which hung from the end of the camera. The script could then be scrolled, enabling Clark to deliver quite long pieces to camera without having to extemporise. Although the crew was well resourced by the corporation the speed of technical improvement was such that their equipment soon seemed slightly old-fashioned. Cameras became smaller, batteries lighter; Kodak brought out a 35mm colour film with double the ASA in 1969.

Filming was spread over four three-month forays, beginning in Italy in 1967 with episodes 4 and 5, on the Italian quattrocento and the Rome of Pope Julius II. By starting halfway through, it was thought, any wobbles could be addressed before the

42

The Autocue machine

pilot. Thereafter the crew jumped around, directed alternately by Gill and Montagnon, back to the Gothic, Carolingian and Dark Ages and forward to the Reformation, baroque and revolutionary periods. Their motorcade featured two Commer vans, two station wagons, a Land Rover (which contained the generator) and several cars. They would cover 80,000 miles in total.

What on earth were they looking for?

3 Sad and Polished

In the end I suppose it is like that superbly furnished *Forsyte Saga*: a long last gathering up, by sad and polished minds, of an Edwardian world-view; an enacting of pieties learned very young and very hard, and now with all the emphasis of a public corporation.

Raymond Williams, *Listener*, 20 March 1969

In the aforementioned notebook in which he sketched out the series Clark followed his first episode list with notes on the 'enemies of civilisation'. He divided these into two: external – 'destruction of war or plague, extreme poverty, a rigid social system' – and internal – 'rigidity, exhaustion, lack of confidence, failure of nerve, hopelessness, disintegration'. Clark found 'civilisation' easier to define negatively than positively. Whatever it was, it was not civility, that 'veneer' of politeness. Nor was it contingent on Progress, that quaint nineteenth-century artefact. It had nothing to do with quantifiable vectors such as increasing literacy or participation in the political process. Nor was its advance marked by easily dated moments of scientific discovery or mechanical invention. An encouraging tonic for some, *Civilisation* left the critic Raymond Williams wondering at the contrast between wearied message and cranked-up medium: an Edwardian swan-song pumped through a Marshall amp. 'I suppose it is to maintain this disjunction between the medium and the message … that we have mandarins and governors,' he speculated.[45]

The relationship between script, music and visuals in *Civilisation* may have been complex, but it certainly wasn't

44

characterised by disjunction. A close study of episode 3, 'Romance and Reality' allows us to see how a typical fifty-two-minute episode of *Civilisation* worked. The pre-title sequence opens with film of stags fighting outside a castle, silent at first, then accompanied by slow medieval shawms. Only then does the word 'Civilisation' fly out from 'behind' us, followed a few seconds later by 'A Personal View by Kenneth Clark'. The 'Sir' only appears in the end credits. Several episodes open with equally silent yet arresting images. For 'The Light of Experience' there is no music at all in the pre-title sequence, and Gill requested that the continuity announcer warn viewers accordingly, fearing that they might adjust their sets' volume. With just eleven pieces of music, 'Romance and Reality' is restrained relative to other episodes. This was probably due to the difficulty of finding music of the correct period. Clark and Montagnon were responsible for selecting the music, and only twice broke their own rule that music never be more than twenty years out of date with the building or object in vision. However rich *Civilisation* sounded, Clark and his directors nonetheless felt guilty for not focusing sufficient attention on music as an art form. They consciously sought to make up for it in episode 9, 'The Pursuit of Happiness', with mixed results. Playing a Bach chorale over the rococo gluttony of Vierzehnheiligen exposes a glaring disconnect between media that cries out for comment.

45

In the pilot Clark speaks in voice-over before appearing in vision. In 'Romance and Reality' as in most other episodes, this is not the case. 'I'm in the Gothic world . . .' he begins. In the first fifteen minutes Clark appears in three locations, outlining the concept of courtly love and emphasising the strangeness of chivalry. 'We've come a long way since Chartres Cathedral . . .', he continues, drawing a contrast with the thirteenth-century world of the previous episode. But his subjects are rarely confined to the fifty- or 100-year slot of historic time covered by a single episode. Chivalry, Clark points out, 'is over now, but it had a long run', and persisted into our own day, in social conventions such as pulling out chairs for ladies. Using tapestries, illuminated books and ivories Clark explores the connections between courtly love and the cult of the Virgin. He turns to consider the fifteenth-century Burgundian court of Jean de Berry, as illustrated by the *Très Riches Heures* of the Limbourg brothers. 'What a dream!', he notes, as if admiringly. Though he clearly does admire the beauty of the world depicted there, he is also able to note that 'it was a colder world for peasants', to consider those outside the privileged elite. Such narrowly circumscribed courts quickly become petrified relics of themselves, he warns. Throughout the series Clark regularly highlights the fragility of such moments of creativity, their tendency to carry the seeds of their destruction within them.

Halfway through the episode Clark deftly turns the focus to St Francis, whose pursuit of 'his lady Poverty' is presented as emerging from the court's chivalric code. This takes us to Assisi and Giotto's frescoes of the life of the St Francis in the Arena Chapel in Padua. The focus now shifts subtly from objects to place, to Assisi, then Siena and finally Pisa. At Assisi Clark speaks to camera, at first from the monastery's colonnade, looking out over the countryside. Then comes one of those extended sequences of film which appear halfway through every episode, always without Clark and sometimes without music. These range in length from two to over two and a half minutes, and were referred to facetiously as 'commercials' by Gill. They provide the viewers with an opportunity to rest, take stock and absorb the atmosphere of a landscape or built environment.

This sense of place is amplified in the second half, where we follow Clark as he moves progressively further outside the monastery, pausing regularly to speak to camera with the monastery behind him. Together with spliced-in film of dogs, turkeys and animals in a nearby farmyard this illuminates Clark's musings on the relative importance of country and city in advancing civilisation (a recurrent theme, also addressed in 'Man: The Measure of All Things') as well as on St Francis's civilised belief in the supreme unity of creation, one which has echoed down to our own day. In discussing the role of cities Clark cannot resist a dig at 'those pre-Marxist innocents, the liberal historians' who used to think that the city-states of Renaissance Italy were democratic.

The mercenaries and merchants who commissioned the frescoes and altarpieces were part of a society built on exploitation. Elsewhere Clark names one of these 'innocents', Henry Thomas Buckle, whose two-volume *History of Civilisation in England* (1857–61) was indeed characteristic of Whiggish meliorism. Clark is no Marxist, however, so there is a hint of nostalgia in that phrase 'pre-Marxist innocents'. While Clark considers both Whig and Marxist history foolish, the latter is dangerous, whereas for him the former is endearing, at worse quaint.

Twenty-five artefacts in all feature in the episode, most of them accompanied by Clark in voice-over. He is clear to signal that he knows the limits of such commentary. 'Look at the heads of the mourning women . . . [in Giotto's Arena frescoes] they need no words from me.' Gill shared Clark's sense that word and image should not be chained to each other. As he wrote to Clark:

> I am convinced that the images must not slavishly follow your argument: they must surround it, extend it, glancingly illuminate it. In particular they mustn't destroy the feeling of place; the ability of the audience to feel that they are joining you in an exciting magic carpet journey.[46]

47

Clark rarely uses conventional terms of art appreciation, and pauses to explain potentially difficult terms such as 'usury'. When he reaches the limits of his expertise, as when he refers to the possibility that chivalry derived from the Arab world, he frankly confesses as much. There are touches of humour, as when Clark notes that the 1,500 dogs reputedly kept by the Duke de Berry are 'too many, even for me', or gently hints at how dull some chivalric romances can be. In the last five minutes Clark introduces Giotto, contrasting the solidity of his vision with the imagination of his contemporary Dante, whose work aspires to the 'heroic sublime', whose ideal of civilisation is embodied in the symbol of light. The episode ends in Pisa, without any attempt to recapitulate or even offer a set of conclusions. Several episodes end with assessments of great individuals whose achievements are only partly explicable as a function of the place and time in which they lived. The treatment of

Shakespeare at the end of 'Protest and Communication' is another
example of this tendency, which denies us the neat conclusion one might
otherwise expect.

Even in such a short and impressionistic summary of one
episode one can gain a sense of the series' ambition, its confidence in the
medium's ability to capture the viewer's attention with an arresting image
and to hold it while the presenter makes connections between different
media and teases out deceptively disposable 'asides' referring to other
questions and ages, including our own. 'Commercials' and frequent use
of rostrum camerawork allowed the viewer the chance to savour works
of art for lengths of time that are unthinkable today. Ambition was
balanced by restraint. Both placed demands on the viewer, albeit in
different ways: comprehension and observation.

The directors seem to have had difficulty deciding whether the
programmes were to be 'clusters of ideas' or 'chronological surveys'.
In May 1967 Montagnon noted that they were to focus on 'general
progression – historic rather than clusters of ideas'. A year later he wrote
to the Head of Arts Features saying the exact opposite.[47] Clark also had
two apparently conflicting models of how to construct the series as a
metanarrative. The first operated using a rock-climbing metaphor:
mankind or 'western man' struggled two steps up the face of Mount
Civilisation, then fell back down. There was no ratchet effect, no way to
cling on and collect one's strength for a further push. Although Clark
occasionally spoke (as in 'The Great Thaw') of 'the ascent of western
man', otherwise he seems to have found this metaphor too progressive
for his taste, too easily hijacked by those who saw 1960s Britain as a
peak of civilisation. 'Man hasn't changed very much' was one of his
mantras (it features in his final credo), and so the series is perhaps more
accurately described as a chemical laboratory. Twelve experiments are
running in parallel. In each retort a civilised solution is bubbling away
happily. Thus Clark could speak of each episode being 'a little drama,
developing a single theme', and concede that his own views as presenter
could appear to differ from episode to episode, rather than illustrating a
single set of convictions.[48] Unfortunately there is also a thirteenth

experiment – 'Heroic Materialism' – that started late, is out of control and which could very possibly blow up, leaving something of a mess behind.

Seen in this way, *Civilisation* is not a single story of 'the ascent of western man' through historical time but thirteen separate stories. Its protagonist's identity is both less stable and less unified. Thus Clark speaks as often of 'medieval man' or 'Renaissance man' as he does of a timeless, constant 'western man'. They are different personae, related to us, but not by any neat Biblical pedigree of 'x begat y'. We confront them as we would a stranger. A family resemblance exists, of course, but it is glancing. Such uncanny similarities are one of the less obvious structures that hold the series together. A tighter, more explicit genealogy of civilised man would have been easier to follow. But it would have denied the viewer the element of surprise at sudden recognition of experience shared between the living and the long dead.

49

Clark and Montagnon discuss a script on location in Rome, as Englander adjusts the lighting

With the exception of Elizabeth Fry in 'Heroic Materialism', Clark's heroes in *Civilisation* were all male. He ignored questions of gender. It would be foolish to claim that in using terms such as 'medieval man', Clark intended to suggest that half the population of past ages had somehow stood aside from the developments he was studying. That said, there is little to support his later claim that the series highlighted how the 'balance of male and female principles' constituted a 'Yin and Yang' that formed the 'basis of civilisation'.[49] Gender was simply not an issue for him or any of the crew, including director Ann Turner. Surprising as it may seem today, back in 1969 it wasn't an issue for British or American critics and viewers either.

Each episode instead focuses on demonstrating how one of these personae created a civilisation in a particular historical period, working within a particular set of social, political and economic parameters, using different men and different media, struggling with different-shaped demons. All are composing poetry, as it were, but in different languages. Some languages lend themselves more easily to the expression of certain human emotions and appetites than others. Though those emotions and appetites never change, the degree to which they are expressed does. A tragic irony provides a mechanism that compensates for any especially large burst of creativity or expression, such as that witnessed in Rome during the High Renaissance. European civilisation, Clark observed, 'reached a point of perfection which led to a revolution and that led to fresh creation. This is a kind of continual pruning. Sometimes root pruning, really.'[50] Extraordinary creativity is more short-lived than ordinary creativity. Hyperbolic feats in expressing a certain sentiment summon destructive demons from their slumbers. This pessimistic calculus wasn't one man's invention. 'I am delighted with your idea of a pessimistic or cautionary ending,' Clark wrote to Gill in July 1967, '[it] will give [episode 5] the same form as 6, and 7.' Or episodes 1–4 and 8–13, he might have added.

Close Enough to Touch

One of the reasons Clark seemed untouchably patrician was because he hated to be touched. In over twenty-five years of working for him his research assistant only kissed him once, and never saw him kiss or embrace his wife.[51] His inflexible stance on camera reminded *Civilisation* editor Roger Crittenden 'more of a statue than a living being'.[52] Gill thought he looked like a tortoise. As his serial affairs (which continued throughout filming) intimated, however, Clark's appreciation of beauty was very physical. Clark might have recognised civilisation when he saw it, but to truly know it, required touch.

Gill later recalled how

> I was filming the exterior of the Royal Naval College [Greenwich] when [Clark] appeared round a corner, moving with considerable haste. 'I know you're busy,' he murmured, 'but just come and look at this.' He took my

51

Clark and Gill

hand (*he took my hand*, this man who never touched anybody!) and rushed me into the chapel. Under the pulpit he stopped and gestured at the asymmetrical sweep of the stairs. 'Aren't those the most perfect curves you've ever seen?', he whispered.[53]

The way in which presenter and camera got to grips with artefacts helped *Civilisation* break the vibrantly coloured surface and explore form and texture. Civilisation wasn't an outline, it was a shape. 'Indeed,' Clark wrote in his early notes for 'The Skin of Our Teeth', 'I would almost define it as the shape given to a sudden outburst of creative energy.'[54]

Although he never commented on it as such, Clark clearly felt it important that he be seen to stroke works of art, to emphasise the haptic as well as the visual. He had stroked pottery on camera in *Is Art Necessary?* and did so throughout *Civilisation*, from the carved hull of a Viking ship in 'The Skin of Our Teeth' right up to the bronze by Henry Moore in the last episode, 'Heroic Materialism'. It is the last thing we see him do, and, combined with a slight smile, leavens his final credo. 'As if to imply that there is still hope,' Clark would later explain.[55] The effect can be very moving, as in 'Grandeur and Obedience', when Clark interacts with Bernini's *Apollo and Daphne*. Clark's hands, the gnarled hands of a sixty-four-year-old man, stroke the equally gnarled, sculpted tree roots. Intertwined, the two momentarily merge, recapitulating the fingers-to-wood transformation that Bernini has choreographed in marble.

The time given to Clark's hands is unsettling, and not just for museum insiders, who might well wonder what sort of curator would allow a television presenter to paw their treasures. Watching it all through the lens, cameraman MacMillan for one was concerned.

I always remember that image of his hand – it's not a rigid hand, its fingers are bent backwards – and he just keeps on stroking it. The film editor should really have cut that down a bit, otherwise it looks almost manic, sexual . . . .

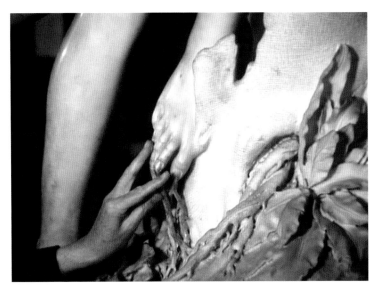

Please Do Not Touch

53

Yet in a way the lens was just an extension of Clark's hand. 'It does seem
to be a fact that the viewer seated in front of his television screen
identifies with the person talking to him,' Gill later wrote, 'and when
this man . . . is seen to touch the prow of a Viking ship, or handles an
ancient cross, so vicariously does the viewer.'[56]

The crew took risks in this belief that the viewer would share
rather than question Clark's enjoyment of texture. MacMillan continues

> If you're showing a piece of work that has been painted, decorated, carved,
> you really have to force the eye of the viewer to take in and notice the
> texture, the colour, the shape. And making the camera go very slow takes a
> bit of courage, because you are teetering on the edge of being accused of
> being boring – 'Oh, this is slow and turgid' . . . so that's the dilemma.[57]

Difficult as it is to describe adequately in words, this shared focus on the
feel of civilisation lent the series much of its impact. It also ensured

The feel of a
Michelangelo

continuity between Clark's pieces to camera on the one hand and the
undercranked interior tracking shots and the rostrum camera stills work
on the other. They matched Clark's intense enjoyment of the artefacts,
stroke for stroke, tracking shot by tracking shot.

54   *Civilisation: A Personal View* is haunted by the ghosts of the
Bloomsbury Group, narcissistic spirits that Clark struggled somewhat
half-heartedly to exorcise. Chief among them was Clive Bell, the group's
chief aesthetic thinker, whose essay *Civilisation* had been published in
1928. In his short book Bell began by analysing what civilisation wasn't,
and came up with a list that looks very similar to that list of the 'enemies
of civilisation' drawn up by Clark almost forty years later. For Bell,
civilisation depended on an elite with the leisure and discernment to
pursue ever subtler forms of 'aesthetic ecstacy'. The majority remained
slaves by necessity; what leisure they had would be spent receiving the
culture diffused by the elite in one-way transmission. Those intent on
civilisation had to concede that democracy and art were incompatible.
'To discredit a civilisation it is not enough to show that it is based on
slavery and injustice, you must show that liberty and justice would
produce something better.'[58] Bell was nothing if not blunt.
'Complete human equality is compatible only with complete savagery.'
He advocated a Utopia straight out of Ayn Rand, in which every

Rostrum cameraman Phil Summers and Ann Turner

2,000th baby would be assigned to the 'aesthete class', the rest becoming drones. Bell's book was heavily influenced by the philosophy of G. E. Moore, whose works left bright young Edwardians such as John Maynard Keynes and Virginia Woolf wondering if the masses who went to the cinema and worked could be considered truly human.

This was the dark side of Williams's 'Edwardian world view'. In *Civilisation* Clark sneered at those 'clever people before the war' who thought that civilisation depended on slavery, ignoring the fact that he himself had been one of their set. He goes on to compare his former friends to 'swans' – poised, mannered and mindless. Yet there is something very Bloomsbury in Clark's musing in 'Protest and Communication' that, 'on the whole', the invention of printing had been A Good Thing. It was just the thing to tweak the noses of leftist academe. Clark was much more circumspect in concealing his belief that democracy had not contributed to the civilising project, except, perhaps, by association with metaphors of liberation that might in turn cause one or two individual geniuses to catch fire. Clark emphasised humanism over humanitarianism. Humanitarianism was, like 'progress', a nineteenth-century invention. Back in 1969 Clark's failure to identify himself with a clear ideological position lay at the heart of younger intellectuals' dislike. Clark was not just old-fashioned in his style of delivery, his failure to commit to a position on the societies whose creative works passed under his gaze was (they held) irresponsible in its lack of commitment. The simple truth is that he preferred to speculate, suggest or propose, trusting the viewers to reach their own conclusions. Having been damned for being evasive and noncommittal in the 1960s, the next generation would damn *Civilisation* for being too confident and categorical. Clark would have enjoyed the irony, one senses.

  Civilisation did its best to contain the elitism of Clark's focus on civilisation as a collection of a few individuals, of 'a minority – often a tiny minority – who, for various reasons, have a temporary power over the majority'.[59] As we shall see in the next chapter, fans made much of his credo at the end of 'Heroic Materialism', sending Clark endless requests for a copy of it. Most of it comprised a list of antonyms, but it ended with a line that confirmed Clark's priorities. 'I cherish men of genius,' Clark says, 'and I cherish a society that makes their existence possible.' Whatever political system, whatever inequalities there might be, any society was to be cherished if it produced one great genius. As Clark noted in the *Radio Times*:

> I am a natural hero worshipper and I early came to the conclusion that each programme must contain three or four heroes, not only because I felt like that, but because the character of an epoch can be more vividly portrayed by describing an individual of genius than by attempting to expound an abstract idea.[60]

When Gill first saw Clark's outline for the series he balked at the cavalcade of 'old warhorses' that threatened to be trotted out.

Montagnon recalls that Clark's initial approach was 'too heroic, he thought that he had to write in a declamatory style, so it didn't come out right'.[61] In the series Clark's hero-worshipping is kept under control. Heroes are conspicuous in the episodes written first (4 and 5), but thereafter they are balanced by other aspects of civilisation. Artists, thinkers and craftsmen are considered less as objects of Clark's veneration and more as illustrations of the 'character of an epoch'. The language used to describe their activities becomes softer. They are incorporated into another strand holding *Civilisation* together: the travelogue. In the best episodes they are presented 'in their element', yet nonetheless mobile. They are not swans. 'The carvers of twelfth-century France resemble nothing more than a flock of dolphins.'

A Sense of Place

Although Clark had presented several travelogue-style shows before 1966, his original plan for *Civilisation* involved a return to the 'still and stool' approach with which he was familiar from his ATV days. According to Gill's account Clark proposed that each episode would begin with 'scene and period setting', then 'not more than three or four key works and places, which are used to illuminate the whole period', ending with a final 'assessment of what the age has contributed permanently to the idea of civilisation'. 'The opening and closing would be in an abstract situation,' that is, a studio. In between, 'he *might* be on location'. Gill gently urged Clark to leave the studio. 'Would it make sense that your exploration of your own ideas of civilisation should be triggered off by your physical return to places that you have thought important in the past?', he asked in February 1967.[62] A few days later a word from his son Colin convinced Clark to cut out the studio.[63] It remained to be seen, however, whether revisiting such sites would lead Clark to make his scripts more personal, addressing another concern Gill had raised on reading Clark's early drafts. Jane Clark saw her role as protecting her husband from television people, and was dead against this. Clark's research assistant Catherine Porteous notes: 'She didn't want K to let it all hang out, in a way that Michael did, he wanted K to be more emotional, and Jane was a counter-weight to that.'[64]

Many of the locations used in *Civilisation* had deep significance for Clark. The floods that hit Florence in 1967 had left many of the crew wondering in what sort of a state they would find the city. As it happened much had been damaged by heating oil, which had escaped from the basement tanks found in many Florentine homes, seeping into marble. For Clark this was the second time he had returned to the city expecting to find precious buildings like the Pazzi Chapel in ruins. As he later told Porteous, he wept when he found the building had survived. When speaking inside the chapel in 'Man: The Measure of All Things' Clark describes how

> when I first came here, fifty years ago, I felt 'this is my true centre'. Well, twice it seemed that they [sic] were lost: once at the end of the German

'This is my true centre'

occupation, and once when the floods came . . . well, so far the forces of destruction have been defeated.

He referred briefly to his own childhood visits to Iona in 'The Skin of Our Teeth', and elsewhere such asides alternated with occasional complaints about recent increases in the press of visitors around such places. This can't help appearing somewhat ironic in hindsight, given how many British and especially American viewers became visitors in the wake of the series. Clark's own response to this effect was characteristic: 'Each man kills the thing he loves.'[65]

Creating a true sense of place in the viewer required careful thought, not least because of the number of locations used. 'I turn up in too many sites in this programme', Clark complained to Gill about 'The Skin of Our Teeth',

> Paris, Nîmes, Pont du Gard, Orange, Mausoleum of Theoderic, S Vitali, West Coast of Ireland, Iona, Aachen, Poitiers and some other I forget; and I can't see any way of cutting any of them out, as I have important things to say in each.[66]

As we shall see later, the way in which Clark kept 'popping up' did indeed annoy many viewers unused to such mobility. Ten years before Compton Mackenzie had been filmed on location in *The Glory That Was Greece*. Compared to *Civilisation*, however, the progress was stately: only four or five 'stations' per episode, in which Mackenzie paused to deliver extensive and unscripted 'reflections' to camera. Clark's itinerary was punishing in comparison, and the 'magic carpet journey' could be unsettling. Whenever Mackenzie addressed the audience from a particular location (actually from Ealing Studios, with back-projection) a map was clearly displayed showing where he was.

There were no maps in *Civilisation*, which caused a certain amount of disorientation among viewers. Montagnon and his fellow directors were nonetheless convinced that it could be made to work:

59

> We reinvented the anchorman and we said something that should have
> been obvious to anyone who had thought about film at all . . . film conferred
> on you the power to be anywhere that you wanted to be and to change from
> one location to another . . . [it] could be done on an idea . . . the idea could
> carry you from one location to another.[67]

The 'carpet' device was pushed even further by Bronowski's *The Ascent
of Man* (1973), and by the time of *The Shock of the New* (1979)
presenter Robert Hughes could start a sentence in New York and finish
it in front of the Brandenburg Gate without a jolt.

    On re-viewing *Royal Palaces* Clark had been 'dismayed by its
quick, even tempo', and felt that he would like 'to give people a few
seconds to reflect at certain points'.[68] Gill and his fellow directors
Turner and Montagnon had agreed at the start that there were to be no
directorial antics, 'none of the tricky angles and fancy zoom-shots which

60

Allan Tyrer

were fashionable at the time and which I had utilised myself in the fantasy-film *The Peaches*'.[69] Something was needed to introduce pauses, however, both to allow viewers to muse on what Clark had just said and to create that sense of place. As Gill observed of the island of Iona, 'certain places do seem to generate an aura beyond the explicable combinations of geography and climate'.[70] The decision was made to introduce long sequences of a particular landscape or architectural setting, without voice-over. Gill called them 'commercials'.

As with the extended close-ups or rostrum camerawork, the 'commercials' showed courageous restraint. This took heroic proportions in a sequence filmed inside a French monastery for episode 2, 'The Great Thaw'. The camera shows monks tilling the soil, tracks a monk returning slowly from the fields, moves the length of the refectory as the monks eat and concludes with a static shot of them moving out into the cloister, single file. One by one they appear, shake loose their

61

A monastic interlude

sleeves and raise their cowls over their heads. The spatial relationships and daily cadence of life in a Benedictine cloister are savoured, for over two and half minutes – an *extremely* long time to go without music, voice-over or the presenter himself. A sequence of even a tenth of the time would be unthinkable today. It takes confidence and faith to attempt such a breathtaking span, to trust that the visuals will hold up without buttressing.

The 'commercials' ran the risk of seeming turgid. That they never did was in large part thanks to the skill of *Civilisation*'s editor, Allan Tyrer. Crittenden worked alongside him on *Civilisation* and observed that

Urbino

> Allan had the ability to surprise you with his editing. He was always able to
> give the director in the film a cut that was smooth and appropriate, but he
> also had that extra ability to shock you in the right way, by moving a
> sequence on, by finding a jagged juxtaposition that gave the film energy.[71]

These sequences did their bit to contain both Clark's pessimism, by
suggesting that, even if the individuals charged with civilising power were
dead and their works imperilled, even if we kept falling back, there would
always be sacred places where western man could recharge and regain
confidence in the possibilities lying within himself. Skellig Michael or
Urbino were not landmarks that had 'served as the backdrop to the events
that made us who we are today'. They were much more important than
that. *Civilisation* dwelt on them, dwelled in them.

Confronting the Infinite

As the full weight of the BBC's expectations bore down and the series
went over its already generous budget, the discipline shown in the use of
location filming seems to have broken down slightly. Presenter and crew
attempted to dramatise. The sixth episode, Montagnon's 'Protest and
Communication', featured three costumed interludes from Shakespeare,
filmed in September 1967 at Kirby Hall, a ruined Elizabethan house in
Northamptonshire: a Macbeth monologue done in voice-over, a speech
from *King Lear* performed by William Devlin, and the gravedigger's
scene from *Hamlet*, featuring three actors around Yorick's grave.
Ian Richardson played Hamlet, while the part of Horatio gave a cameo
to Patrick Stewart. The penultimate episode, 'The Fallacies of Hope'
(directed by Gill), opened with a special-effect sequence which saw
Clark dramatise the romantic rebellion. Summoned by strains of
Beethoven, Clark stormed out of the trim world of the 18th century,
leaving the secure confines of Osterley House to confront a roiling sea,
which the magic of television brought right up to the colonnade of that
fine Adam-designed house in landlocked Middlesex.

63

64   Patrick Stewart and Ian Richardson

The Shakespeare and the 'Osterley-on-Sea' episodes were the only two sequences that Clark regretted having done. As he observed in the *Radio Times*, 'the transition from a documentary to a theatrical manner of speech makes me feel uncomfortable'. The sea sequence 'seemed to me a harmless *coup de théâtre*, which would not be taken seriously, but on the whole I regret it, as everything else in the programmes was authentic'.[72] Williams agreed, describing the Shakespeare episodes as 'an expensively dressed schoolboy's error'.[73] Whether they are better seen as ludic sallies or simply mistakes, they do raise important questions of whether there were aspects of civilisation that this kind of television could not convey. They also invite discussion of what is being presented – a series of artefacts, quotes and objects that illustrate a lecturer's thesis, or, as the subtitle 'A Personal View' might suggest, a more intimate rendering of Clark's own vision. Viewers clearly responded to the sense of being in a discussion with a learned man. How could that sense be upheld while at the same time presenting dramatised episodes that project images from Clark's imagination?

It is clear from their correspondence that the directors struggled to come up with a plausible explanation as to how these sequences would work. As already noted, at the start of the project they had agreed that there was to be no 'fancy work' on *Civilisation*. Gill himself was critical of the inclusion of costumed actors in documentaries such as Russell's *Elgar*. One has the sense that Gill was determined to go ahead, but needed to come up with a party line for the crew to use should these episodes subsequently run up against criticism. A month before the Shakespeare scenes were filmed Gill wrote to Montagnon arguing that

> The dramatised moments must appear to arise from Clark's mind. They are summoned up by him as visual illustrations and personifications of the words, in the same way that he can summon up at will illustrations from anywhere to fit his argument.[74]

65

A harmless *coup de théâtre*?

Hence each of the three Shakespeare interludes is introduced by Clark, if somewhat allusively. Devlin's *Lear* monologue thus illustrates Clark's comparison of Shakespeare with Montaigne, a similarity he believed he had been the first to note.

In Shakespeare's case 'instead of the essay, there's the urgent communication of the stage . . .' Clark says in voice-over, just before a bearded Lear lunges out of a blank doorway. The camera tracks him across a courtyard, eventually revealing a musing Clark, in vision but out of focus, leant up against a column in the middle distance. Devlin walks out of vision, the film cuts to Clark in close-up, whereupon he looks up, smiles and finishes his sentence: 'Pure Montaigne . . . with a difference.' Clark then moves on to the second theme of the episode, from the 'isolation of the individual' brought about by the 'barbarism' unleashed by religious wars to the related trend of 'the laicising of the intelligentsia'.[75] We then have Eric Porter voicing the 'Tomorrow and tomorrow' speech over a slow tracking shot of blank windows, a sequence which also ends by 'discovering' Clark, who continues talking.

The third and longest scene (Yorick's grave) forms the end of the episode. Clark has already had his say, suggesting that we are to take the scenes as illustrations of his point: that for all the 'tragic split' which followed the Reformation, 'the human mind has gained a new strength by outstaring this emptiness'. Clark seems to have had an intense dislike for tidy soundbite endings, gifted as he was in tossing off thoughts that stick in the mind. Had he made this uncharacteristically clear and succinct final statement *after* the grave-digging scene, it might have borne an inflection of pride. Placed before the scene, it seems less pat. There is still plenty of 'outstaring' for the viewer to do, as Richardson delivers his final line (on how the dust of Caesar might serve to plug a draught) and the credits roll over more shots of Kirby Hall's ravaged façade, with an additional soundtrack of a whistling wind. *Civilisation*'s treatment of Britain's greatest poet and dramatist is anything but a celebration of 'Merrie England' or an Elizabethan golden age.

In 'The Fallacies of Hope', the dramatic episode comes at the very start, and again Clark is presented as hearing voices in his head. The episode dispenses with the usual pre-title sequence, and goes straight to a short title sequence featuring Tchaikovsky's *Francesca da Rimini* played over shots of Auguste Rodin's bronze, *The Gates of Hell*. It then cuts to close-up of the plasterwork inside the library at Osterley, music replaced by silence, except for a ticking clock. The camera pulls back to show the entire room, into which Clark walks. 'A finite, reasonable world . . . symmetrical, consistent . . .' he says in voice-over, turning at the mantelpiece to add, with a stately frown put on for effect, '. . . *enclosed*.' Such worlds can, he says, become 'a prison of the spirit', which demands movement. Clark then unbends, and returns to his usual conversational tone, with humorous asides, hand gestures, a stroke of the mantelpiece. But then he lowers his head, we hear music start up, as if being played outside. When Clark lifts his head, he is acting once

Channelling Beethoven

more. The sudden contrast to his usual manner can be painful to watch. Ostensibly 'channelling' the Romantic spirit, Clark, it is all too clear, is delivering lines:

> And what is that I hear? That note of urgency, of indignation, of spiritual hunger? Yes! It's Beethoven, it's the sound of European man once more reaching for something beyond his grasp. We must leave this trim, finite room and go to confront the infinite.

Clark turns, opens the door, and leaves. We then see him crossing the outer hall. Characteristically, the 'summoned' Clark ambles to confront the infinite with one hand in his pocket. We then see him outside the building, from behind, looking down from the colonnade on to the 'sea' below. It is night, but all is lit by an eerie blue light as Clark, brows taut and voice raised against the tempest's roar, continues his speech: 'We've a long, rough voyage ahead of us, and I can't say how it will end, because it isn't over yet. We're still the offspring of the Romantic movement and still victims of the fallacies of hope.'

Beethoven now plays over film of pitifully small waves crashing on a shore. Crittenden cut the sequence and remembers searching Gill's film of a Cornish beach in vain to find even slightly impressive waves. The sea-effect at Osterley had to be sent out to a separate lab. Trying to get the exposure of the two films (that of the sea, and that of Clark) to match took a lot of work. Finally the 'storm' recedes, and we see the same Cornish beach. It is day, and we find Clark there, more sensibly dressed in a tweed topcoat. 'This escape was also an escape from reason.' Order is restored.

There was to have been a second, more elaborate dramatisation of Beethoven's *Fidelio* later on in the same episode, where in the final cut a succession of black-and-white stills and archive footage appears, one short sequence of stills or clips for each of the European revolutions. The country and date appear one by one on screen, flying up from the 'back' of the screen, newsreel fashion. This revolutionary roll-call starts with 'France 1830' and proceeds through nine others

Osterley-on-Sea

before reaching 'France 1968' and 'Czechoslovakia 1968' – colour news
footage is rendered in black and white to maintain visual continuity.
We then find ourselves back outside the prison door at Vincennes.
A musing Clark manoeuvres mournfully through the door, then speaks
in his conversational tone: 'As far as freedom was concerned I'm afraid
that recent revolutionary movements haven't got us far forward.' This
sad truth is delivered with something of a lilt in the voice, poised on a
knife edge between *Schadenfreude* and genuine sorrow.

Gill originally planned to include new film of a group of extras
struggling out of a mine into daylight. This would tie in with the *Fidelio*
chorus laid over it, sung by prisoners escaping to freedom. The mine
idea was originally Clark's, and Gill proposed that Clark could stand
watching 'on the opposite edge':

This could hardly last the time that we would need to run the music, and I
am thinking of insetting into the shot of them climbing up the steps images

70   Revolution newsreel

from later revolutionary movements. This would begin like a star shell from
the centre of the picture and slowly spread outwards, so that by the time we
were into the present century they would have completely blotted out our
extra prisoners. Then, when the last image – perhaps from Prague 1968 –
fades, we would be back on our original location, now empty, for you to do
your summing up.

For reasons that remain unclear this idea was never tried out.

　　All these sequences highlight the difficulties of accommodating
drama and music in *Civilisation*. There was music throughout the series,
of course, but it was usually not alluded to in Clark's script, nor were the
pieces or even composers identified, even in the closing credits. The BBC
was flooded with letters asking what this or that piece of music was.
In episode 9, Clark stands in vision and informs us that this particular
episode will be especially dedicated to music, and we are told in advance

that we are to hear Bach played over a sequence of the interior of Vierzehnheiligen. Clark names Beethoven's *Fidelio*, too, before the revolution sequence.

These sequences all involved a certain amount of toying with Clark's role as presenter, assigning him almost supernatural powers to summon up a storm or actors. I have noted how these sequences forced Clark to move rapidly between two vocal registers: that slippery 'after-dinner conversation' voice and a much more authoritative 'voice of God' used to impose a particular mood. The latter is employed in other episodes, at the start of 'The Great Thaw', for example, which opens grandly with a 'God' line delivered out of vision: 'I'm in the Gothic world . . .'. Clark resorts to this register sparingly, partly because he was uncomfortable with it, and partly because the images absolved him of the need to. They set a mood, translating the viewer to a particular place in time and space.

71

Jacob Bronowski

Here is one revealing contrast with the present-day image of
the series. *Civilisation* is held to be characteristic of the 'presenter as
hero' model, which might lead one to assume that sequences like those
described above would be the norm, rather than the exception.
Bronowski's *The Ascent of Man* does have a strong narrator who pulls
the viewer and visuals in his wake. Everything is subordinated to the
guru's preternatural magnetism, which works in seeming defiance of
Bronowski's breaking every rule in the book. His eyes leave the camera
for long periods, his lines admit incredible pauses, at times he even turns
his back on the camera. Though powerful, the visuals in *Ascent* never
really establish their own presence, rarely communicate with the viewer
without the presenter's mediation. In *Civilisation* presenter and visuals
were evenly balanced, despite the fact that the directors thought of
Clark in guru-like terms:

> We'd got a guru figure and the question was, how to use this guru figure to
> best advantage. I think we would have only driven what he had got to say
> right out of the window if we had tried to dress it up too much.[76]

With the exception of these sequences, they did not dress Clark up too
much. But, as already noted, they did do a lot to create film sequences
that are independent of Clark's imagination or argument. Indeed, at
some points Clark's script seems to be reacting to the film we have just
seen, as a fellow viewer, rather than a lecturer who has choreographed
everything, and who stands off in the wings while the professionals
carry out his instructions.

Looking back over the making of the series, Clark, Gill and
others all remarked on how well the crew had worked together.
To quote Gill, Clark's 'new breadth of vision'

> came partly through working with a team of very different opinions and
> becoming as it were a spokesman for them, so that an exchange with Bill
> Paget the grip while walking back from a location would flavour the way he
> wrote the next day's piece.[77]

The only episode that Clark admitted had caused problems was the last, 'Heroic Materialism'. The episode opened with a helicopter shot of Manhattan, a freeway interchange and other shots of New York. Stravinsky plays in the background. Clark first appears on the Staten Island Ferry. New York, he notes, took roughly the same amount of time to build as the medieval cathedrals did. From a distance, it looks 'celestial'. 'Closer to, it's not so good.' Superficially impressive, sordid underneath would seem to be his general approach to the civilisation in which we live.

At the end of the previous episode, 'The Fallacies of Hope', Clark spoke next to Rodin's monument to Balzac. The monument should, he stated, inspire us to fight all the forces that threaten to impair humanity. Though the list is long, Clark reels it off with a relish that invigorates. We can eliminate them all, he suggests, every one: 'tanks, tear gas, ideologues, planners, computers . . . the whole lot'. This spirit seems to have departed Clark in 'Heroic Materialism', which dwells, sadly, on the ironies of civilisation. Yes, we abolished the slave trade, but only to 'dehumanise' millions at home, in factories. We have broken through the Victorians' cruel cant, but have paid the price in the loss of our belief in virtue and worthiness, which have been reduced to 'joke words, only used ironically'. Set against such a script, the chirpily cut

73

'Closer to, it's not so good'

'tanks, tear gas, ideologues, planners, computers . . . the whole lot'

steam-engine sequence that follows a few minutes later seems jarring, a hollow joke.

The episode then considers Seurat, Renoir and Van Gogh, none of whom rise to heroic proportions. And then it enters the 20th century, represented by Jodrell Bank Observatory's Lovell Telescope, a typewriter typing, dials, Concorde and a rocket launch. Gill was aware of the hackneyed nature of such a sequence, and Tyrer's editing slips in an atomic bomb test and Stuka divebombers, injecting some much needed edge – and, of course, ambivalence. As Crittenden puts it:

> I do feel that there is a pessimism, [Clark's] pessimism, but certainly the image juxtapositions were very much about the fact that what we call progress is often backwards, that wherever the progress of humanity has been forward, you can always find two steps back with every one step forward. I think it was important not to have a sequence of images that was too simplistic, too one way or the other, but to at least to imply – both with

Brave New World

images and against his words – the sense that we should be careful not
simply to congratulate ourselves on our achievements when at the same time
human society can be said to be not improving in any way, shape or form.[78]

The episode only really pauses amidst the moonscape of Denys Lasdun's
brutalist architecture at the University of East Anglia in Norwich, with
slow, tracking shots that struggle unsuccessfully to strike root, to suggest
any sense of place. Originally Clark was to have finished up at Giza in
Egypt. Gill's idea was to have Clark deliver his lines, then cut away to a
sunset over the pyramids. Stills from previous episodes would then play,
by which time the sun would have reached the horizon.

    Civilisation instead ended inside Clark's own library at his
home, Saltwood Castle, though this location would not have been
recognised by viewers. By this point in 'Heroic Materialism' the viewer
is in need of reassurance. Apart from that final gesture, Clark's stroking
the Moore bust on his way out the door, we are denied it. For a series

A touch of hope?

derided as patronising, *Civilisation* fights shy of having the last word.
The episode has Clark doing something he did not wish to do: pin down
his own convictions. Adopting his characteristic perch against a table,
Clark pauses to confide:

> At this point I reveal myself in my true colours, as a stick-in-the-mud. I hold
> a number of beliefs that have been repudiated by the liveliest intellectuals
> of our time.
>
> I believe that order is better than chaos, creation better than
> destruction.
>
> I prefer gentleness to violence, forgiveness to vendetta.
>
> On the whole I think that knowledge is preferable to ignorance, and I
> am sure that human sympathy is more valuable than ideology.

Clark's credo is largely a list of antonyms, though he goes on to add a
belief in courtesy, in 'the God-given genius of certain individuals' and in

Clark delivers his credo

the higher natural unity of man and all other creatures. Much in demand by fans (who wrote in asking for copies), as an attempt to sum up the series the credo is a failure.

Clark is saying very little about his own beliefs, and setting up a ludicrous straw man. What man or woman *wouldn't* prefer knowledge to ignorance, creativity to destruction, politeness to rudeness? The closer one considers it, the less coy Clark's reference to himself as a 'stick-in-the-mud' appears – and the more calculating. It flatters the viewer, of course, to consider themselves alone together with Clark on some final bastion of civilisation, surrounded by the vulgar hordes. Many middle-aged, middle-class viewers nervous of rioting students, trade unionists and immigrants may have read it this way. It is disarming, of course, of Clark to marginalise himself as superannuated, as a historical curiosity. He acknowledged the gap between his approach and the Marxist one that was then gaining profile in academe and out. But his credo sets up a false dichotomy between a monolithic 'sympathetic civilisation' and 'intellectual barbarism'.

The credo is (as he admitted himself) a collection of banalities. 'It contains nothing striking, nothing original, nothing that could not have been written by an ordinary harmless bourgeois of the later nineteenth century.'[79] Coming at the end of thirteen episodes that have taken us from the storm-ravaged Atlantic coast to Rome and back, it does indeed sound bathetic, and reads even worse. A nuanced series that refuses to grasp the easy definition, that dodges truisms and remains alive to the unpleasant ironies of civilisation (its dependence on warlike impulses, for example) suddenly lurches from colour into black and white. That curious qualifier 'on the whole' highlights the foolishness of the exercise. Clark's hands are not up to chiselling words into tablets of stone. In this one matter, one wishes Gill had listened when Clark refused to come down the mountain. Apart from episode 1's 'What is civilisation?' segment, the credo is the only part of the script that viewers interviewed for this book could quote. The series' reputation has suffered as a result.

Technology has advanced to the point that one can safely assume that the film that makes the directors' final cut is indistinguishable from that seen on the viewer's television screen. In 1969 the situation was much more complicated. Translating 35mm colour film to a colour UHF signal was complicated, and gave ample opportunities for meddling by technicians who were not above adjusting sound, contrast or even individual colour levels in real time, shot by shot. Any director who cared about how their film came across had to be ready to fight back. But where to make one's stand? Unable to be in all places at once, one had to decide between the Control Room, telecine, or the TARIF machine. This last was a collection of oscilloscopes whose name stood for 'Technical Apparatus for Rectifying Indifferent Film'. When *Civilisation* went out for the first time the BBC threw a lavish viewing. Clark, Gill, Montagnon, Tyrer – everyone was there. Except Turner. She was in the control room, protecting *Civilisation* from the barbarians.

4 A Television Milestone

Call it the epic poetry of television, call it a hymn of praise to the dignity and orderly genius of man, call it a symphony of beauty, erudition, and brilliant colour photography. Call it what you will, but BBC2 have produced yet another television milestone.

Manchester Daily Mirror, 24 February 1969

Expectations were high before 'The Skin of Our Teeth' was broadcast on BBC2, at 8:15pm on Sunday, 23 February 1969. Crittenden recalls the buzz in the Ealing Studios canteen, a certain envy of those fortunate enough to be working on what all realised was a different kind of television. Meanwhile outside the corridors of the BBC Huw Wheldon was doing his best to talk up the forthcoming series. It *was* a landmark, one that could only have been achieved by the BBC, 'the basic fact being that we are probably uniquely good at this kind of venture'.[80]

The BBC's 'Viewing Barometer' was calculated using diaries submitted by 2,250 viewers. The barometer estimated what percentage of the UK population over five years of age (50.5 million) was watching. A glance at these barometers makes it clear that when it came to viewing audience *Civilisation* was no *Forsyte*, although its launch coincided almost perfectly with the latter's final episodes. *Forsyte* had begun back in January 1967. Episode 25 went out at 7:25pm on *Civilisation*'s first Sunday, ending at 8:15pm when *Civilisation* started over on BBC2. The season finale the following week reached a staggering 36 per cent on the barometer. 'The Skin of Our Teeth' reached 1.7 per cent, and later

CIVILISATION

THIRTEEN PROGRAMMES ON BBC-2 IN COLOUR

WRITTEN AND NARRATED BY SIR KENNETH CLARK

'A ravishing
cavalcade of
beautiful things'

Sunday broadcasts hardly went higher – while they reached 1.8 per cent
for episodes 9–11, such differences were well within the range of
statistical error. There was no spike for the concluding episode, and
figures for the weekly repeat on Fridays at 9:05pm were more or less
identical. Higher figures were reached in Spring 1971, when *Civilisation*
was repeated on BBC1. Now scheduled for 9:20pm on Tuesdays, in
1971 *Civilisation* started with a very respectable 10 per cent, falling to
around 8 per cent in the following weeks. On 9 March *Civilisation*
('Man: The Measure of All Things') was the most watched show on air.
For half an hour at least, until ITV's *Bless This House* started.

A broader look at the barometers allows these figures to be put
in context, to see how *Civilisation* fitted into the primetime landscape.
Apart from warhorses like *Coronation Street* (25 per cent), typical

audiences for a popular variety show like ITV's *This Is Tom Jones* were around 15–20 per cent. On BBC1 Cilla Black was still finding her feet, struggling to match the phenomenal *Black and White Minstrel Show* or the *Rolf Harris Show* (29 per cent!). In terms of comedy and drama, BBC1 had two hits in *Dad's Army* and *Z Cars* (both around 20 per cent), but was otherwise struggling to compete with several glossy spy/investigator series that achieved cult status: *The Saint*, *The Avengers* and *The Champions*. Apart from Westerns, it is striking to note how little American television was in fact being broadcast, at a time when television was often blamed for undermining British culture.

Civilisation's disappointing figures were a result of colour's novelty. Only one in every 200 television sets was able to receive BBC2's colour signal. Few of the crew had colour televisions themselves. It is revealing that when the 1969 Grand National was simulcast on BBC1 and BBC2 in March the former got 30 per cent – BBC2 only 1 per cent. In his 1977 autobiography Clark could therefore claim with some justice that his ATV programmes were more widely seen and exerted a greater influence in England than his later series ever did.[81] In 1969 BBC2 programmes rarely received more than 5 per cent of total audiences, and the highest BBC2 figure for the period was a mere 9 per cent, for *The High Chaparral*. There was some concern that BBC2 might end up being a sort of television Third Programme, featuring highbrow documentary strands like *Horizon* and one-offs on Anton Bruckner. Even on BBC1, arts magazines were not doing much better. *Monitor*'s successor, *Omnibus*, was hovering around 2–3 per cent. Meanwhile *Civilisation*'s unlikely twin, *Monty Python* (which followed *Civilisation* every week during its 1971 repeat), was garnering around 5 per cent.

Those who did watch, however, were very impressed by what they saw. In addition to its barometers the BBC also commissioned audience-research reports on specific programmes: in *Civilisation*'s case, episodes 1, 2 and 9 for the 1969 BBC2 broadcasts, with a fourth report on 'Heroic Materialism' commissioned during the 1971 BBC1 repeat. Members of their Viewing Panel were asked to score programmes and invited to submit comments. In practice only around 5 per cent of panel members (about 100 people) took up the invitation to give *Civilisation* a mark (from A+ to C–). The resulting figures were used to calculate a 'Reaction Index', or RI. Here *Civilisation* performed well, starting high at 79, then dropping to the mid-70s before reaching an outstanding 85 for 'Heroic Materialism'. Popular shows like *Dad's Army* scored in the 60s, though, here again, *Forsyte* broke all records. It is doubtful whether any programme ever recorded a RI higher than the 93 received for the 1969 season finale.

This audience research suggests that very few found *Civilisation* patronising or stuffy. No more than two or three of the 109 who reported on 'The Great Thaw' found Clark slightly pompous or 'too academic':

> Sir Kenneth Clark made a very favourable impression . . . . Indeed, most thought that his quiet, scholarly manner, love of his subject, 'mind-boggling knowledge', and ability to convey it to the layman without appearing in the least patronising, made him a first-class cicerone, a Housewife declaring: 'Had the programme been three hours long, I would still have sat through it enthralled.'[82]

Several observed that the series 'was clearly going to be a "must" for the next few weeks', Clark had interested them in a topic they candidly admitted to having previously found unappealing. They also admired the photography.

Opinions were more divided on the music. Gill was aware of the important role music could play in making the 'duration for the length of a particular take . . . appear natural to the viewer'. At the same time he was also aware of the potential harm it could do, by insisting on a certain emotional response: ' "Now feel this," it says with a tremolo of inappropriate violins.'[83] In *Ways of Seeing* Berger brilliantly illustrated this effect by including two different sequences of details taken from Caravaggio's *Supper at Emmaus*, one set to Italian opera with rapid camera movement and a more reverent one set to a chorale. Viewing Panel members and several of those who wrote in to Clark found the music too loud or insistent. Part of the blame may lie in the technicians adjusting levels during transmission. It must be admitted, however, that the music does occasionally cut Clark's commentary off in a somewhat rude fashion. Ultimately one has to conclude that the amount of music featured in *Civilisation* was yet another area in which the audience's expectations were challenged. Back in 1967 Gill had warned Clark of the danger of '*over*-richness', which he linked to television's urge to cram in too much.[84] Music was one aspect some viewers found 'over-rich'.

One of the wearisome criticisms that continues to be levelled at the series is that it somehow assumed that western civilisation was the only civilisation. There is something insulting about ascribing such a belief to a man who clearly admired Islamic, Egyptian, Indian, Chinese and Japanese literature and art. Clark himself presented programmes on the Egyptian and Japanese civilisations before he turned to 'the west', and he made it explicitly clear in the series and in related media appearances that he was not asserting the latter's primacy. He did assert that the history of western Europe displayed the contrast of civilisation and barbarism, the clash of self-confidence and doubt and the rise and fall of different aspects of civilisation with a force that the history of other regions could not match. 'None has shown the same restless eagerness to build and to destroy; the same ingenuity, the same vital power of recovery.'[85] 'All one can say,' Clark noted in a separate interview, 'is that the Eastern civilisations never went down to the bottom the way Western Europe did. So they never had the chance of climbing gradually up.'[86] If that was an orientalist compliment, it was a back-handed one: Europe won this competition because it kept falling backwards, over and over again. And Clark didn't have to summon up a barbarian Other from outside his European enclave to drag them back. The barbarians were inside the gates, inside us.

Related criticisms based on the geography of *Civilisation* made at the time and since also fall short. In the years after 1969 the question 'Where was Spain?' was heard, almost as often as 'Where was the rest of the world?', even in Venezuela, on the other side of the Atlantic.

83

When the series was shown in Caracas the Iberian lacuna developed into a minor diplomatic incident, one the British ambassador worked hard (with help from Clark) to address.[87] The series itself was indifferent to such score-keeping. Civilisation was not the hostage of nations.

'Is nationalism the necessary enemy of civilisation?', Clark had written in the red notebook in which he sketched out his first thoughts for the series. 'The answer is very nearly yes.'[88] Though small Renaissance courts such as Urbino were celebrated as providing a home for civilisation, Clark was concerned not to overstate their role. He candidly confessed his own dislike for courts, and initially hoped to leave out Versailles. He was somewhat more willing to concede civilisation to be an urban phenomenon. Ultimately, though, civilisation did not crave a certain soil. It could not be cultivated. Whether it sprouted on a bare rock in the Atlantic, in the dark, narrow canyons of Renaissance Florence or flat marshy polders of Golden Age Holland, civilisation was always a surprise.

84

The Art of Travel

Civilisation was a pilgrimage. Had Clark remained in the studio the series would have had a genuinely patronising sense of a presenter despatching the viewer to visit certain places, then summoning them back to receive a succinct summary of their significance. Hard as it is to appreciate today, taking the presenter outside the studio was a big step in 1969. It represented a loss of authority, the threat of exposure. Not every presenter was up to it. This explains why *Monty Python* found it so rewarding to do sketches in which a presenter and his desk were put on the back of lorries, placed on beaches and in other unlikely places. It was funny because it seemed so unlikely. In 1971 only one-third of Britons had ever travelled abroad, and it seemed slightly incredible to have a presenter appear in a dozen different locations in the space of fifty minutes. To borrow a *Python* line, it was 'something completely different'. Viewers could be annoyed by the way in which the presenter kept 'popping up' in different places. They lost track of which building was where, and wanted a map to be shown to help them keep up. Newspapers and the *Listener* tried to make it all easier to follow by publishing maps of each episode's locations, under the title 'This week Sir Kenneth visits . . .'. Here again, *Civilisation* was '*over*-rich'.

In *Temples* Clark had occasionally spoken dismissively of the tourists that spoiled the atmosphere of the world's greatest sacred sites; a common enough complaint for someone who had travelled widely before the war, when only the wealthiest went abroad. The episode on St Mark's, Venice ended on a stuffy note, in an unhappy bit of writing that is typical of the ragged endings which truncated several of Clark's ATV programmes:

> A constant stream of tourists flows wearily round – stout, moist, undecorative – chiefly interested in feeding the pigeons. 'Oh, for one hour of blind old Dandolo!' However, I mustn't start quoting poetry [Byron's *Childe Harold*]. It's the surest way to bore an audience – anyway it's time. Time, gentlemen, please.[89]

85

There is something of this in *Civilisation*. In 'The Worship of Nature' a family is briefly shown enjoying a walk in the Lake District, indifferent to the po-faced voice-over bemoaning the effect of such tourists on the area. At other times Clark was able to see the parallels between the well-worn tourist trails and the medieval pilgrimage routes, to interpret them as a positive sign that a shared sense of sacred places and artistic values did in fact exist. As he noted in his 1966 Granada Lecture, a new humanism might one day emerge from the 'jostling' around tourist sites.

Such complaints can seem hypocritical today, in so far as *Civilisation* can surely be assigned some of the 'blame' for the foreign travel boom that began in the 1970s. It was, as already noted, a travelogue; viewers spoke of Clark as a 'cicerone'. Other factors contributed to make 1969 something of a turning point. The same year saw the first widebody jet, the Boeing 747 go into commercial service for the first time. Concorde's maiden flight took place on 2 March. It was

broadcast live just a few hours before 'The Great Thaw' went out.
Concorde was itself shown in the montage of clips which brought
'Heroic Materialism' to an end. In 1970 Concorde and the 747 would
carry thousands of Americans across the Atlantic in search of the places
featured in *Civilisation*. The BBC stimulated home demand with
another 1969 first – *Holiday '69*, a travel advice programme that
continued for many years, helping many Britons dip their toe in the
unfamiliar world of foreign holidays.

Clark inevitably became irritated with the jetloads of admirers
who passed through London on '*Civilisation* tours'. As he explained to
an executive at one American PBS affiliate:

> Of course I am always glad to meet people who have enjoyed my *Civilisation*
> programmes but in the last few months quite a number of universities and
> travel agencies have taken up the idea of *Civilisation* tours in Europe and
> they all tell their parties that in the course of the tours they will meet me.

Concorde

Discord

> If I acceded to all their requests it would take up quite a lot of my time and
> would tend to exhaust my benevolence, so I must ask you to forgive me if I
> include you in a general ruling not to meet people who are coming to
> England on *Civilisation* tours.[90]

Clark had unwittingly launched a new invasion of 'stout', 'moist' and
sometimes 'undecorative' people. Not that everyone was complaining.
The city of Urbino knew a good thing when it saw it, and threw the crew
a lavish dinner at the end of filming there. As they anticipated, it put
their city on the map.

Trying Not to Get Screwed

Clark had been very unwilling to share his convictions in *Civilisation*,
and only agreed to perform his credo at the end of 'Heroic

Materialism' under pressure from the directors. The sequence filmed inside and outside one of the new universities, the University of East Anglia, was on the surface an optimistic comment on the massive expansion of access to higher education that had begun in 1962, when only 4 per cent of school leavers had gone on to further study. These students were, Clark says, better educated and better fed than any generation before them; a source of hope. In his 1966 Granada Lecture he had been far less positive. 'Much as I admire the bright and beautiful people whom I see in the new universities, I fancy it will be a long time before they can bring spiritual and intellectual order out of present chaos.'[91]

In 'The Fallacies of Hope' Clark looked down on revolting Parisian students and wondered 'what precisely do they hope for?' In a programme full of revolutions the '68 students seemed jejune and unco-ordinated. During breaks in filming crew members followed the crowds, observing police brutality and tear gas at first hand. MacMillan recalls watching the students pontificating inside the Opera. They raided the wardrobe for suitable historic costumes. Revolution was a fancy-dress party, but the outfits didn't quite fit. 'It was rather amusing,' Montagnon recalled. Nobody took it that seriously – except the Clarks. They were 'really rather nervy'.[92] 'We've a long, rough voyage ahead of us,' Clark promises at the start of the episode, 'and I can't say how it will end, because it isn't over yet.' In '68 Paris, Clark wasn't waiting to see what happened next. Montagnon managed to buy enough petrol on the black market to get them all across the Belgian border.

But that does not mean that Clark saw *Civilisation* as a political statement, as a reassertion of values that the 1960s generation had supposedly dismissed. As he observes in 'Heroic Materialism' the records of civilisation were inviolate, pre-political. 'There they *are*, you can't dismiss them.' Other commentators were less chary of interpreting the series as a timely reminder of the need to appreciate and cherish western civilisation. Clark's close friend, warden of All Soul's College, Oxford John Sparrow observed in the *Listener*:

Another French Revolution

> In more ways than one, western civilisation resembles the pound sterling.
> We assume its significance, its stability, and its superiority over all its
> rivals. Our confidence in the pound has been undermined for some time
> past. Today the value of western civilisation is also being challenged, and
> there are people about who would like, if they could, to destroy it. I don't
> mean by the atomic bomb, or the Cold War, or any kind of external attack.
> The threat I am thinking of comes from within.[93]

Student protest, post-modernism and pop culture were interpreted by
many as examples of that cynicism and failure of nerve which Clark had
identified as two of the enemies of civilisation.

A leader in *The Times* of 17 May 1969 echoed Sparrow's
language. This was the first time *The Times* had devoted a leader to a
television programme. Entitled 'How Like an Angel', it saw the series as
giving the lie to Clark's gloomy Granada Lecture of 1966. Television
could tackle 'solemn subjects'. The series showed what the BBC
could do 'when the sights are set high and kept high'. Praising
Clark's 'urbane, unemphatic delivery', it saw the series as offering
a much more appealing image of civilised man than the 'rather self-
centred, if not downright selfish' one portrayed by Clive Bell in his book
Civilisation. Clark, it claimed, offered two key lessons for the future.
He had demonstrated that western society could retain its faith in the
dignity of the individual; in the past, periods of great materialism and
brutality had also witnessed the birth of humanitarianism. It also
showed that man could move forward when he grasped and upheld
'humanity's moral sense and belief in the authority of a higher power'.
Whether these lessons were being learnt was as yet unclear. 'And now?',
it was led to ask, 'Is western civilisation renewing itself or becoming
empty of meaning?'

Civilisation had entered the realm of politics. Roy Jenkins had
already yoked 'civilisation' together with 'permissiveness,' both in the
1959 Labour manifesto (*Civilized Society*) and in the new freedoms he
introduced during his Home Secretaryship (1965–7). *Civilisation* was
taken by many as an excuse to take the word back. A more permissive

culture had left students and artists to toy unsupervised with barbarous reflexes that were just as potentially destructive as the atom bomb they sought to ban. It had spawned a generation that ignored hard-won lessons and experience. In 1969 the voting age was lowered from 21 to 18. Some middle-aged fans wrote to Clark saying that they felt all teenagers should be made to watch. Here Clark and his fans invoked the spirit of the Victorian Matthew Arnold, whose *Culture and Anarchy* (1869) had critiqued a tendency to associate progress with a permissive, 'fay ce que vouldras' ('do as you like') mentality.

On screen and off, Clark was highly sceptical of the student revolutionaries of 1968 and their hopes of radically reshaping the world. In his final remarks Clark stated that the failure of Marxism had left western Europeans with nothing but Heroic Materialism. 'And that isn't enough.' Marxist critics of the New Left were understandably unmoved by this. Marxism had not failed. As Stefan Collini has noted, the type of criticism that Williams and others enshrined in the new universities as 'Cultural Studies' was locked within a 'hermeneutics of suspicion', the suspicion 'that most forms of cultural activity are essentially a disguise for the fact that Somebody Is Trying to Screw Somebody Else'.[94] Williams believed that the creation of ITV had been a 'planned operation from the United States' masquerading as a 'popular' movement.[95] Not that he held the BBC to be truly representative, either. To paraphrase Williams's remarks in the *Listener*, an ostensibly 'public corporation' had allowed its considerable resources to be prostituted by the worst kind of Edwardian critic, 'that still figure, secure in his property as a consumer of other men's work'. The third episode may have moved Williams to pay some compliments, but they were back-handed ones:

> I like picture postcards, and this collection, aided by some camera movement, was delightful. The commentary, also, was less bizarre than hitherto, though at the same time no more authoritative. The observations on detail are often unconvincing; the historical generalisations neither here nor there, since in that old dinner-table style they keep slipping away into

91

> mannerism. But where I had been roused to argument, talking back at the screen, in the first two programmes, I now found myself letting the decorated pages turn . . . . The structure of feeling is very open and familiar, but since the style is informal it keeps slipping away while there is so much worth looking at.[96]

There is simply too much for him to do, so he 'just' looks. And to look is to 'give up', to fall into a trap, in so far as all images are political statements, rather than aesthetic experiences to be enjoyed for their own sake. Clark was at ease with late nineteenth-century aestheticism, with the Paterian view that 'aesthetic ecstacy' could be an end in itself. He was comfortable admitting that *Civilisation* was intended to entertain, and that it therefore necessarily contained generalisations that, 'in order not to be boring, must be slightly risky'. That, after all, was 'how we talk about things sitting around the room after dinner'.[97] Williams was nervous of the rich, entertaining fare *Civilisation* offered; satiation dulled the critical faculties in a way that felt deliberately contrived. Although he was not addressing this particular series when he wrote it, one is reminded of Williams's reference in his 1974 book *Television: Technology and Cultural Form* to 'a single irresponsible flow of images and feelings'.[98]

Williams's book emerged from the experience of watching several days' worth of American television in a Florida hotel room while recovering from a transatlantic cruise. The book uses the word 'flow' to describe the way in which advertisements, idents, news and entertainment programmes meld. The analysis is predominately technical and institutional; again, Williams is overwhelmed by the images. He simply can't keep up, and hardly attempts to assess how people actually consume television. Instead much of the book attempts to reinject human agency and choice into a history of the medium. Television is not, he demonstrates, simply a product of technological progress, nor is its development simply an outlet engineered in response to certain emotions and modes of expression. Writing in the *Listener* Williams had described *Civilisation* as belonging to those programmes

Conceived for
mainly visual
reasons

'obviously conceived for mainly visual reasons', a phrase suggestive of a profound naivety, but which may have been intended as meaningful criticism.[99]

Someone so visually dyspeptic was an odd choice for a television critic. But, to quote Collini again, 'after a certain point [Williams's] opinions were printed because he had become the sort of person whose opinions were printed'.[100] Williams's views nonetheless anticipate the approach of Berger's 1970 BBC2 series *Ways of Seeing*, which peeled off the artifically preserved veneer that had supposedly been applied to fine art in order to 'make inequality seem noble and hierarchies seem thrilling'.[101] Like Williams, Berger cast Clark as one of the 'few specialized experts who are the clerks of the nostalgia of a ruling class in decline'.[102] All the purposes to which we were putting art were abuses, forms of advertising that imprisoned the viewer in pleasing fantasies. Berger manipulated images himself, hanging a 'No Trespassing' sign in Gainsborough's *Mr and Mrs Andrews*, and employing shocking and highly effective cross-cutting. Yet he seemed unable to suggest a replacement for the civilisation he attacked, to suggest how we were to engage with art once we had been informed of its manipulation. The series consisted of just four half-hour shows, that were, like *Civilisation*, broadcast twice, and then widely sold as 16mm film. Berger followed *Civilisation*'s lead in producing a book. The book's

93

success has far overshadowed the original series, which despite its importance and visual power has never been released on DVD.[103]

Williams and Berger were not the only ones who critiqued *Civilisation* as representing a disappearing generation's nostalgic farewell to the certainties of their youth. The *Sunday Times* art critic John Russell went further in associating the series' 'vespertinal tone' with a particular generation of curators and art experts:

> The civilization Clark describes is one that has had its day and will not be seen again; there is a note, almost, of apprehension in the way he passes it in review . . . . If I am right in this, posterity will recognize in *Civilisation* the understated *Liebestod* of an attitude to life that was initiated by Walter Pater, codified by Bernard Berenson, and propagated by the generation of esthetes, art historians, collectors and museum men who held sway in the Western world between 1914 and 1965. This generation had no higher praise than 'life-enhancing'; it ranked each civilization in terms of the art-objects it left behind; and it had no doubt at all that the supreme periods of art had been and gone. The great men of the past were all contemporaries, for the generation of which I am speaking; but that their own contemporaries could be men of the same stature they found hard to credit. Values, for them, were fixed and final; standards were immutable.[104]

This reading chimes with anecdotal evidence suggesting that the series' relative unpopularity among art historians and curators today may reflect the same individuals' rejection of the series as undergraduates in the late 1960s.

Every generation of students challenges the nostrums of its professors to some extent. From 1970 the rise of the 'the new art history' saw an attempt to study a much broader range of objects, as a way into the politics of class, gender and (eventually) race. When its disciples thought of 'civilisation', they were reminded, not of Clive Bell's 1928 book, but Freud's *Civilisation and Its Discontents* of 1927. As late as the 1930s the 'old' art history that enshrined connoisseurship and 'life-affirming' aesthetic values had only secured a toe-hold in academe,

Berger

however. There were no degree courses available outside the Courtauld Institute, itself founded in 1933. To its promoters within the new universities, therefore, the 'new' art history could appear to be the first 'real' art history. This search for a professional identity combined with Clark's semi-detached position relative to both 'new' and 'old' art history made the reception of *Civilisation* particularly fraught. Had he truly been a retardataire figure it would have been easy for young art historians to dismiss *Civilisation*. Unfortunately for him, Clark could seem to be inventing his own 'new art history' by the very insistence with which he stated (in episode 1) that the history of civilisation was *not* the history of art, and by his repeated jibes at the 'experts'. Though the teaching of history shifted from high political to socio-economic explanations under the influence of E. P. Thompson and Williams in the 1960s and 1970s, there was less at stake for history, a more established discipline. Today's history professors remember the series more fondly. To the new art historians, however, *Civilisation* was something of a menace, a body of connoisseurship and irresponsible appreciation that was (they told themselves) dead – but which looked worryingly spry when rendered in living colour.

Even in Oxford, which had yet to begin teaching art history, Clark was a figure of fun to undergraduates who went on to hold leading positions in the art world. In 1969 Giles Waterfield was a student at Magdalen College:

> Back then we found what we perceived as the sweeping generalisations and pretensions of the series laughable. While watching the odd episode in the Junior Common Room we took turns to amuse ourselves with comic impressions of Clark.[105]

Waterfield went on to serve as director of the Dulwich Picture Gallery. Among his fellow Clark impressionists was a future art critic for *The Times*.

The series was well received by the *Burlington Magazine*, the bastion of 'old' art history. The *Burlington* ignored the 'new art historians', but paid enough attention to know that they didn't like Clark much. It also recognised that they were not alone in their hostility:

> Over the years, Clark has engendered a certain, often latent, hostility in art-historical circles. Jealousy is part of it, and so is suspicion, not only of the eloquent style but also of the generalizations, the sweeping analogies, the formulae into which he fits, with an ease sometimes bordering on facility, whole worlds of artistic activity. There is also an understandable resentment. Ever since *The Gothic Revival* was published over forty years ago, his books and articles have been peppered with tiny, lethal jabs at the inadequacies of the scholarly temperament.[106]

Clark was not really one of their own. The *Burlington*'s obituary of Clark, for example, wrote of 'his rare incursions into formal art history'.[107]

'We thought we were invincible'

While filming, the crew had faced the unrest of 1968 with equanimity. 'We thought we were invincible.'[108] Although the series went down very well with the relatively privileged audience able to watch it, among Marxist critics equanimity equated arrogance. *Civilisation* stumbled into an academic turf war, arousing a certain amount of resentment that continues to colour its reputation today. The response was warmer across the Atlantic, but no less political.

5 Civilisation in America

Secret of its appeal has three parts:

1. The films are the quintessential travelogue; beautiful, exciting!
2. The approach to the subject is interdisciplinary, offering 'a history of life-giving beliefs and ideas made visible and audible through the medium of art;' stimulating, thought-provoking!
3. The man, Kenneth Clark, projects a rare personal quality and provides the ultimate punch of the series by communicating a keenly felt sense of values – values which help put today's world in perspective and speak encouragingly of the future.[109]

'You and *Civilisation*', WMVS Channel 10 Milwaukee promotion

Civilisation had a much larger audience and a greater impact in America than in Britain. In London, Clark told a group of reporters in 1970, 'kind people stop me in the streets and talk about the programme ... but they're always Americans'.[110] It was first seen in a phenomenally successful series of screenings at the National Gallery of Art in Washington. The gallery then rolled out a nationwide loan scheme which brought the film to an estimated 10 million viewers. Only then was the series broadcast by the Public Broadcasting Service (PBS). PBS had been created under the 1967 Public Broadcasting Act to facilitate co-operation among the many educational stations that had sprung up around the country since 1952, when the Federal Communications Commission (FCC) had set aside 242 UHF channels for such use. The service makes no programmes itself, but was established to provide

America's Cold War comforter

a framework within which affiliates can share the programmes they produce, thus encouraging the creation of programming with nationwide appeal. In the late 1960s it gave Americans a 'fourth network' to compete with NBC, CBS and the relatively new ABC. It also appealed to new corporate sponsors, who spotted an opportunity to burnish their image as 'good neighbours'.

Combined with new federal funding channelled through the Corporation for Public Broadcasting (CPB) as well as massive contributions towards start-up costs by the Ford Foundation and other private bodies, the advent of PBS injected a degree of centralised co-ordination into a broadcast model that had hitherto interpreted its public-service responsibility in localist terms. Affiliates now signed up to a set PBS menu of primetime programmes, most of which came from traditional bastions of the East Coast establishment, such as Boston (WGBH) and New York (WNET, formerly National Educational Television). Helped along by $350,000 of CPB money, *Civilisation* was the entrée on the first such menu, and so played a crucial role in defining the relationship between the centre and the periphery. By relaying *Civilisation*, PBS affiliates not only benefited from a national media campaign trailing the series, but also gained a fund-raising opportunity. Viewers who enjoyed the series were encouraged to become supporters, paying subscriptions to become co-owners of 'their' local station, receiving a guide to the series (or, if they were especially generous, the book) as a thank-you gift.

Federal funding and news-based documentaries drew PBS into national politics, particularly when President Nixon threatened to cut CPB funding in an attempt to keep public television (which he saw as politically hostile to his administration) local and relatively low-profile. *Civilisation* was on screens during the height of this crisis, and its popularity made it a figurehead: to oppose PBS was to oppose 'programmes like *Civilisation*'. At a time when there were few PBS poster children Kenneth Clark was sent forward to join Big Bird on the front line. Clark's reaction on being yoked to the ten-foot yellow bird off the new hit children's show *Sesame Street* (1969–present) is unrecorded. A complex rhetoric formed around such flagship series. Although the costs of buying, promoting and broadcasting such shows were borne by private foundations and corporations, 'programmes like *Civilisation*' were, each station declared, made possible by 'viewers like you'. In both rhetoric and reality it proved challenging to reconcile increasing dependence on funding by Xerox (who spent $750,000 buying and promoting *Civilisation*) and other firms with PBS's sense of itself as television by the people, for the people.

The rapid expansion of public television stations and the birth of PBS clearly had an enormous impact on how Americans watched

Civilisation. For many it was the first PBS programme they had seen, the first time they had tuned into their local public station. With its roots in educational and university-outreach television, PBS was overtly 'improving' and pedagogic. The 1962 Educational Television Facilities Act that funded start-up costs for public stations had followed a widely reported May 1961 speech by the FCC's Newton Minow. Minow had slammed commercial television as a 'vast wasteland' of sub-standard programming. From the start PBS therefore defined itself as an 'oasis', as possessing qualities that commercial television lacked *sui generis*. *Civilisation* appeared in a context that already suggested fragility and threat, even before Clark appeared in front of Notre Dame. The atmosphere was charged in a way it would have been hard for British viewers to understand. Though largely unknown in the US, Clark was carrying a far greater load of expectations and preconceptions in America than at home.

Of course, the BBC's founder Lord Reith had been mapping the 'wasteland' of commercial culture long before Minow. Like PBS, BBC2 was a newcomer to the air. But the BBC was far more confident, especially after the 1962 Pilkington Report. Education was only part of its perceived remit, and ultimately secondary to providing news, drama and comedy. In 1969 public television in the US had no news programmes, no comedy and few dramas. Although it would create news shows that rival anything on BBC television (*NewsHour*, 1983–, above all), PBS only attempted a home-grown drama once, and never tried comedy. PBS was earnest television. Even *Sesame Street* was promoted as social welfare, with volunteers touring housing projects and proposing the establishment of 'viewing centers' in the ghettos. PBS sold *Civilisation* as a positive, life-enhancing experience, one to be shared with others, often as part of a formal programme of adult education backed up by special educational packs available from stations. Each episode was followed by a five-minute filler in which a cleric, scientist or other intellectual was interviewed on the ideas discussed in that episode. This enthusiasm for the educational value of the series was far less obvious in Britain, and must have seemed quaint or simply confusing to its makers. Like most runaway successes, at some point *Civilisation* left the rails that had been prepared for it.

     Civilisation was not the first BBC export success on American public television. That honour belongs to *The Age of Kings* (1961). The BBC had produced black-and-white, studio-based films of Shakespeare's history plays for broadcast in 1960. Given new titles (*Henry V* became *Band of Brothers*), US rights were sold to NET for $250,000, the purchase underwritten by the sponsor, the Humble Oil and Refinery Company, which later became Exxon. Special introductions were added featuring Frank Baxter, a University of Southern California professor already known for his lectures on the Bard, which he illustrated using wooden models he carved himself. The next great BBC import was *Forsyte* (1969). It was the success of *Forsyte* that inspired the creation of *Masterpiece Theatre*, which opened with the BBC's *The First Churchills* (1970). With *Forsyte*'s Susan Hampshire as the Duchess of Marlborough and Alistair Cooke taking the place of Baxter as *Masterpiece* compere, *The First Churchills* went out alongside *Civilisation* on PBS's core schedule.

     Even if it wasn't the first British export to American public television, *Civilisation* and the shows which followed in its wake – Alistair Cooke's *America* (1972, aired in US 1973), Jacob Bronowski's *The Ascent of Man* (1973, aired in US 1975) – provided PBS with ready-made documentaries that were inexpensive, yet which nonetheless had high production values. Formats and a surprising number of staff would later be borrowed as well, the science documentary strand *NOVA* (1974–) being based on BBC's *Horizon*. It all helped seal a three-way symbiotic relationship between the BBC, PBS and the sponsoring corporations. Sales abroad provided the BBC with a valuable revenue stream and evidence that their product was not irredeemably highbrow. The popularity of BBC documentaries and dramas with a well-educated, managerial class only made them more appealing to the corporations who funded them, even if this success caused others to question whether PBS was honouring its commitment to serve the less fortunate. For such firms sponsoring a single series like *Civilisation* or a strand like

Alistair Cooke

103

Masterpiece Theatre represented phenomenal value for money. Firms could pose as public-spirited while reaching a wealthy and educated audience resistant to traditional advertising – all for a fraction of the cost of a television spot on a major network. Only occasionally did they question whether PBS hadn't gone too far in its Anglophilia, as when *Civilisation* and *Masterpiece Theatre* were deliberately *not* translated as *Civilization* and *Masterpiece Theater*.

It could seem that the infant PBS had been taken over by tony British imports that presented a certain idea of Britain. The original title for *Masterpiece Theatre* had been *The Best of the BBC*. Hosted by Alistair Cooke and Vincent Price respectively, *Masterpiece Theatre* (1971–), renamed *Mobil Masterpiece Theatre* (1995) and *Mystery!*

(1980–) played host to *Upstairs, Downstairs* (LWT, 1976–7),
Brideshead Revisited (Granada, 1982), *The Jewel in the Crown*
(Granada, 1984), *Inspector Morse* (Granada, 1987–2000) and similar
series. Britain was Oxbridge, Empire and murderous country villages
where everyone wore tweed. The original mission of PBS had been to
broadcast educational shows that appealed to as wide a demographic as
possible. Though undoubtedly amusing, the *Sesame Street* spoofs of
BBC posh – *Monsterpiece Theatre*, hosted by 'Alistair Cookie' (Cookie
Monster in a dressing gown) were worrying, suggesting a self-conscious
broadcasting claque laughing at itself.

Meanwhile, back in Britain, there was an odd form of cultural
feedback, even as the BBC insisted that American sales never influenced
its programming decisions. BBC programmes were distributed in the US
by Time-Life Films (later Time-Life Multimedia), who helped finance
America and *The Ascent of Man*. The 1980s heritage boom saw Patrick
Wright and others note the risk of Britain morphing into a theme park
for Americans in search of locations used in hit PBS shows.[111] A quarter
century on, Castle Howard still has one of its main rooms devoted to the
making of *Brideshead*, while Oxford plays host to *Inspector Morse*
tours. Once again, this television-inspired American tourism started
with *Civilisation*. There is insufficient room here to offer a detailed
history of American public broadcasting, to assess its impact on Anglo-
American relations, corporate America and British self-perception.
Civilisation is nonetheless an excellent place to start thinking about
what such a history might look like.

Playing to the Gallery

Civilisation's beachhead in its invasion of America was the National
Gallery of Art, Washington. Ann Turner had established links with its
assistant director, J. Carter Brown, in the course of picture research for
Civilisation. Brown was an early advocate of film as a means of
rendering museums and their treasures more accessible, and produced

J. Carter Brown and Clark

The American Vision, a series of programmes tracing the history of American painting from the 17th century. In 1969 he became director of the gallery, and soon negotiated the loan of a set of prints of *Civilisation* to show in the gallery's 300-capacity auditorium. Screenings began 2 November and became a runaway success. Initially one episode was shown twice a day for a week, with three screenings on Saturdays. Entry was free, and seats were allocated on a strictly first-come, first-served basis, and so celebrities like Jackie Onassis had to wait in line with everyone else. According to the *National Observer* those jostling for a seat included 'government workers on their lunch breaks and peace marchers in town for the Nov[ember] 14 mobilization'.[112]

In the second week Brown responded to demand by showing episodes 2 and 3 back to back. Still the line stretched outside and around the museum's exterior. Brown later recalled:

> Our first realization of the problem came that first Sunday night, when
> instead of a normal attendance of four or five thousand people, we had over
> 20,000 people show up at the Gallery, and the corridors outside our
> auditorium were close to panic level. We then went on Red Alert, and pushed
> our exhibition of the films to the maximum available limit, showing each film
> all day, every day, continuously. This we did for thirteen weeks, and even then
> there was such a hue and cry about 'Civilisation' coming to an end, that I . . .
> made a public appeal for funds, so that we could buy our own print.[113]

The January 1970 issue of *Vogue* reviewed the series, describing it as
'marvellous, chatty, a window opened by a man whose mind is an
orchard of plums'. In the summer of 1970 Carter Brown put on a special
set of screenings for interns, laying on a rock band named Gambol for
the opening reception. Even among this younger audience, demand was
high enough to require an additional weekly screening. By September
1970 over 250,000 had seen the films at the National Gallery, and
gallery attendance figures were up more than 50 per cent on the same
period the previous year. The film was also shown to government and
military personnel at the State Department, CIA and at the White
House.[114] Senator Robert Kennedy wrote to Carter Brown thanking him
for enabling the Senate to view the series.[115]

    Everyone wanted to see Clark when he travelled to Washington
to help promote the series. On 18 November 1970 he was the guest of
honour at the National Gallery, where Carter Brown awarded him a
medal for Distinguished Service to Education and Art at a lunchtime
ceremony, which was followed by a press conference. Gill was already on
the East Coast scouting locations for his next series, *America*, and so was
able to attend and film the ceremony. The expectant crowd had once again
spilled out of the room, lining the central atrium and corridors. As Clark
walked into the room they began to applaud, some reaching out to grasp
his hands as he went by. Back in 1958, in one episode of *Is Art Necessary?*,
Clark had drawn a contrast between the true artist and the commercial
performer. The former was like a renowned cellist: withdrawn, self-
contained, totally focused on the work of art. The latter pushed himself

forward, madly gesticulating, begging the public to love him. Clark did an impression at this point: eyes agape, voice quavering, imploring hands waving. His disgust for both performer and audience was clear.

Ten years later, he could not cope with being treated as a celebrity himself.

> It was the most terrible experience of my life. All the galleries were crammed full of people who stood up and roared at me, waving their hands and stretching them out towards me. It is quite a long walk, and about half way through I burst into tears at the sheer pressure of emotion . . . I had somehow to control myself, stand on a platform, listen to *The Star Spangled Banner* and make a speech . . . I did it, and was proud to have done it . . . I then went downstairs and retired to the 'gents', where I burst into tears. I sobbed and howled for a quarter of an hour. I suppose politicians quite enjoy this kind of experience, and don't get it often enough. The saints certainly enjoyed it, but saints are very tough eggs. To me it was utterly humiliating. It simply made me feel a hoax.[116]

107

Gill shared Clark's astonishment at the spectacle.

> People were packed throughout the gallery: Clark had to progress slowly from room to room to reach the podium in the West Sculpture Hall; the dense crowds rose to their feet at his passing so that he was like a surfer borne forward on a rising surge of adulation.[117]

One sixty-five-year old lady told a reporter for the *Miami Herald* that she had vowed not to leave 'until I touch him'.[118]

'The procession down the gallery was very disturbing,' Clark would later write in a letter to Brown. 'I felt like a man who is supposed to be a doctor, walking through a crowd of earthquake victims who are appealing to him for medical supplies.'[119] At the start of his short speech accepting the medal he openly confessed that 'ever since the programmes first "took on" I've felt a terrible fraud'.[120] In a later letter to Brown he added:

The faithful await

Of course I am greatly touched by the response to the series. I suppose that what disturbed me so much at the National Gallery was partly the physical impact of a crowd of admirers, and partly the fear that I would burst into tears on the platform and be unable to speak.[121]

Clark's tears may have reflected two conflicting emotions, anguish and pride. In Britain the series had been politicised on the one hand by pundits like Williams and Sparrow or else admired as a testament to the talents of the great artists, architects, thinkers and poets it celebrated. 'The Americans are an enthusiastic people,' Clark noted at the time 'in England the reception of the series was curious. Many of the criticisms were hostile; some of them, written by the more intellectual reviewers, were vituperative.'[122] The audience prior to the 1971 BBC1 showing was, as we have seen, very small. In America, *Civilisation* was viewed from the very beginning as a statement about the human condition and a celebration of its potential. It seemed to offer a clear narrative of progress to a nation reeling from Vietnam and teetering on the edge of nuclear holocaust.

Clark's tears may have reflected his anguish at having been cast in a role he felt unable to fill, as America's Cold War comforter. Denied any more promising material, thousands of people had wilfully misinterpreted the series, choosing to overlook its pessimism. They found in it 'something to believe in' – but that was only half of what Clark intended the series to contain: 'I hope that [it] will also give people a healthy scepticism.' In crossing the Atlantic Clark had moved from a public discourse shaped by Williams's extreme scepticism to one dominated by equally extreme credulity. 'I believe,' Clark's speech continued, 'that one of the purposes of education is to balance scepticism and belief.' What a hope!

Among his family and intimates it was quite normal for Clark to cry. As Porteous recalls, 'he was easily moved to tears by something very beautiful, or something that took him back nostalgically to things'. As it happens, Gill also had a propensity to cry when confronted with beautiful works of art. Clark and his wife shed tears of pride when their daughter Colette won admission to Oxford University. Clark may well have been moved by a sense of achievement, of pride in himself. Other members of the crew sensed that he loved the attention he received in America. 'He was vain,' Montagnon notes, 'but redeemed by the fact that he knew it better than anybody.'

109

The gallery's extension service also lent prints of the films to other educational institutions across the country. BBC Radio and TV Enterprises recorded ninety-five hirings and sales of more than forty prints to universities, schools, museums and colleges, including the public library of Newark, New Jersey (site of some of the worst of the 1967 urban riots), the University of Chicago, Choate and the US Naval Academy. *Civilisation* was screened everywhere, even on the US Navy's nuclear submarines. One person who attended a screening at the town hall of East Orange, New Jersey wrote to thank Clark:

> Among the superb works of art that you brought to us as examples of
> civilization at its highest moments of creativity, not the least is your own
> superbly wrought film series to an audience starved for just such

emanations of light at a dark time in history. If this sounds somewhat extravagant – let me tell you that I have never seen a more attentive audience than the one at Town Hall. No one even sneezed or coughed, despite the season – and not a few wept.[123]

God Bless Xerox

History documentary series were something new on American television. The nearest precedent was John Secondari's ABC series *The Saga of Western Man* (1963–6). Secondari thrust the viewer into costumed reconstructions of key moments in the history of western civilisation, though the subjects tackled ranged widely, and there was no attempt to sustain any overarching narrative or chronology. For an ill-favoured Cinderella network struggling to establish parity with its mighty sisters NBC and CBS, *Saga* was ambitious. It met with considerable acclaim in its first season, before Secondari's love of the dramatic seemed to get the better of him. The 1966 'Beethoven: Ordeal and Triumph' is typical in having no narrator in vision. Slow tracking shots move around Viennese palaces and the composer's garret, candles are alight, places set, sheets rumpled – but no sign of any people, apart from a few ghostly, backlit actors, whose faces cannot be seen. Secondari's voice-over is supplemented by a fictional monologue attributed to Beethoven himself. Voiced by David McCallum, these words are laid over shots intended to create an impression of being inside the composer's head.

The end result is a show that appears poised, and which largely avoids cliché, apart from the French Revolution, which is signified by a rock thrown through a window and peasants waving pitchforks. In attempting to depict the deafness that gradually isolated Beethoven, however, Secondari's script rapidly descends into farce. McCallum's voice wonders why he cannot hear his clock (which we see in close-up), utters hackneyed imprecations to God ('Why did it have to be my ears!? Why not my legs?!') only to give up and shout at himself. Apart from some background information regarding patronage networks there is no attempt to explain the historical or musical context, nor is there any attempt to justify Beethoven as a composer of great music. Secondari focuses relentlessly on his personal ordeal, yet asserts that this story 'born of one man's desire to overcome his fate' is 'part of the saga of western man'.

Attenborough had not thought of American markets when planning *Civilisation*, even though the BBC/ITV co-production *Royal Palaces* (1966) clearly had been made with an American audience in mind. A glossy brochure was prepared, and paid off: NBC bought the rights to *Palaces* for £100,000 (it had cost £38,400 to make).[124] But the BBC did not see any chance of selling *Civilisation* until after the series had gone out. Only then was a brochure created with a foreword by Wheldon. Time-Life Multimedia had a special one-hour compilation created, entitled '*Civilisation*: A Preview'. Thirteen fifty-minute episodes had to be squeezed into a commercial hour. This truly unenviable task of editing fell to Roger Crittenden. A bevy of Time-Life executives was sent over to supervise this process, he recalls, whose main concern was finding places suitable for station idents and advertising. Thanks to sponsorship from Xerox, the result was aired nationwide on NBC at 6:30pm on Tuesday, 8 September. This undoubtedly helped advertise subsequent broadcasts of the complete series on PBS. Sadly, this film does not seem to have survived, on either side of the Atlantic.

Xerox spent a total of $750,000 (*c*. £4 million/$8 million today) on *Civilisation*. The corporation paid the BBC/Time-Life $300,000 for the full series, and spent a further $450,000 promoting it – $336,000 of this went to buy one hour of primetime on NBC in which to show the aforementioned preview, alongside six minutes of spots for Xerox itself. The rest went on print advertising. 'Watch *Civilisation*, the TV series it took 1600 years to produce. Presented by the Xerox Corporation' ran the byline in a sumptuous two-page magazine spread. Further advertising trailed the series as '13 hour-long television essays on Western man, his art and ideas'. The corporation devoted a special number of its house journal, *Xerox World*, to the

111

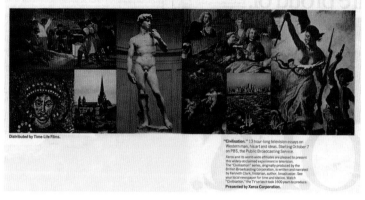

After 1600 years civilisation gets its own television series.

Brought to you by Xerox

series, complete with a pull-out-and-keep guide summarising each
episode. It explained the appeal of such sponsorship to large
corporations in 'vast wasteland' terms.[125] Xerox's vice president in
charge of communications David Curtin was quoted by *TV Guide* as
being 'stopped cold' by commercial television's lack of interest in
quality programming 'of the kind we like to associate ourselves with'.
While the ratings had been a disappointment, Curtin felt 'it was a *good*
audience for our purposes'.[126]

Xerox had previously sponsored documentaries including the
series *Of Black America* and *Luther* (both 1968). It gave $1 million to
fund the 1973 production of *Sesame Street* in Mexico (as *Plaza Sesamo*)
and Brazil (as *Vila Sesamo*). On one level Xerox saw PBS as an
opportunity to appeal straight to upper-level managers who made the
decisions about which sort of photocopier to buy for their offices. As a
1974 handbook on American Corporate Social Responsibility (CSR)
demonstrates, however, such sponsorship went far deeper. It represented
just one of a total of seventeen programmes addressing social exclusion,
from projects working with ex-offenders to free language courses for
Mexican immigrants. Xerox also provided its employees with the

chance to take a year's sabbatical on full-pay to volunteer, demonstrating a disinterested and precocious concern for CSR.[127]

Other sponsors of PBS programmes included General Foods, Polaroid, Du Pont, Philip Morris, Mobil, IBM, GTE and Sears-Roebuck (through its foundation). The sudden increase in such sponsorship in 1970 – $3 million from just nine companies – worried *Advertising Age* as well as the FCC. Some FCC members thought that controls on how often sponsors' names could be mentioned on PBS were not strict enough. Business sponsorship of PBS as well as of art exhibitions and other art forms was very new, however, and the critical response was warm. 'Would it be sacrilegious to bless a corporation?', asked Frank Judge of the *Detroit News*. 'No? All right; God bless Xerox!'[128]

PBS affiliates broadcast *Civilisation* from 7 October 1970. Alistair Cooke had written a special introductory article for *TV Guide*, full of the sort of gee-whiz humour Americans had first experienced when Cooke hosted the arts magazine *Omnibus* (CBS, 1951–6).[129] *Civilisation* was scheduled on Sunday evenings at 9:00pm, right after the television chef Julia Child. She made bouillabaisse to celebrate. On some PBS stations, such as KQED San Francisco, it appeared after *Night Line* with William Buckley, Jr. Each episode was repeated on Wednesday evenings. In America *Civilisation* was safely out of reach of meddlesome Television Centre's technicians. But North America's colour-TV standard, NTSC, was just as much of a problem as TARIF. Attenborough considered it 'garish and appalling'.[130] Translating from the European PAL system to the much poorer American one was difficult. Indeed, NTSC was known as 'Never The Same Color' to insiders, and internal WNET Engineering Evaluation Reports referring repeatedly to 'Variable skin tones – host' suggest that there were difficulties.[131]

113

Viewers Like Him

Many PBS affiliates issued companion guides or promotional material advising viewers on how to watch the series. WMVS Milwaukee organised a series of 'Viewing-Discussion Groups' in several locations. These would, it was promised, 'serve to renew an awareness of what is precious in our history and our culture and to update interest in enlarging our knowledge of who we are'.[132] PBS had encouraged such a response in the five-minute fillers that followed each episode. WNET president James Day interviewed a series of guests, each chosen for their expertise in an area thought relevant to that particular episode. The dancer and choreographer José Limón commented on 'The Hero as Artist', the *Washington Post*'s society columnist addressed 'Romance and Reality', a Jesuit 'Protest and Communication'. Denis Hayes, co-ordinator of Earth Day was a more promising choice for 'The Worship of Nature'. One can't help regretting that Kurt Vonnegut backed out of discussing 'Heroic Materialism', although Alvin Toffler, author of *Future Shock* (1970) must have been an interesting fall-back. These fillers have been lost, and so it is difficult to assess what contribution they might have made. Even so, one senses that *New York Times* critic Jack Gould was right: 'The decision to add a five-minute epilogue was a mistake. The mood with which original producers elect to end a program should not be disturbed.'[133] Yet such fillers were also tacked onto later series. Those for *The Ascent of Man* (aired on PBS, 1975) were hosted by Anthony Hopkins.

In addition to the book of the series, PBS stations also advertised a more affordable $1 companion. Written by the American curator and lecturer Richard McLanathan, *A Guide to Civilisation: The Kenneth Clark Films on the Cultural Life of Western Man* featured a short biography of Clark, episode summaries, a listing of the art and music featured, a glossary of historical terms and suggestions for further reading. Affiliates encouraged viewers to buy the guide and use it within viewing groups made up of family members or neighbours. If family members or neighbours were not interested, they could ask their local librarian to recommend like-minded individuals to them. 'If group-viewing isn't for you, solitary reading and viewing and thinking your own long thoughts can', a WMVS brochure promised, 'be a very pleasant and worthwhile way to continue your education.'[134]

In a more formal academic setting *Civilisation* proved a godsend to professors eager to liven up that freshman warhorse, the 'Western Civ.' course, often derided as a 'Plato to Nato' romp. A special *Civilisation* course was laid on at the University of Virginia. This was probably explained by the fact that the campus, designed by Thomas Jefferson, was featured in 'The Smile of Reason' (episode 10). But several other colleges, especially small ones such as the Rochester [New York] Institute of Technology's College of Continuing Education and Marywood College in Scranton, Pennsylvania also made screenings the focus of special courses.[135] University extension departments at the University of Wisconsin and elsewhere were even more enthusiastic. The University of California and Miami-Dade Community College created a *Civilisation* 'telecourse' in 1979. By that point they had already produced a course for *The Ascent of Man*. Xerox had also produced a study guide for *America*, distributed to Social Studies teachers in secondary schools.

This outburst of educational earnestness was confusing to Clark personally, and seemed totally alien to the British mindset. Earnestness and enjoyment were not mutually exclusive however. Among Clark's papers is a file marked 'Nice Fans. To Keep'. It contains far more letters from America and other foreign countries than from Britain. Many American fans noted 'the sense of wonder that comes from being alone with one's teacher ... in an atmosphere of tranquillity', even if they admitted having to retreat to a corner of the house to escape the noise of their teenagers' music. Clark's mannerisms do not seem to have put them off. Patti and Harry Brown of Illinois sent Clark a Christmas card with a confession:

115

> I must let you know, that some of us here have fallen in love with you, personally, your smile, the way you purse your lips and your inflection of voice, as you narrate the program 'Civilisation' – without you the program would fall flat.[136]

Many American viewers found Clark's long-term perspective a source of comfort. 'We had the first atomic bomb go off at the threshhold of our adulthood,' noted one fan, 'and via the mixed blessing of TV – we have been inflicted with the myriad of hysterias accompanying contemporary life.'[137]

Word of Williams's and other British critics' response had apparently spread, even reaching Miami, where Doris Altier heard of it:

> I have read some criticism from English 'intellectuals' about this program, on the grounds that it 'talks down' to the audience and that it is too elementary. That may be true to those who were fortunate enough to grow up with some sort of cultural background and then to go to the finest schools of higher learning. But to someone like me, in the middle age of life, a child of working-class parents, your program *Civilization* was a thrilling experience and an awakening of interests I never dreamed I had . . . . To me, you are a warm friend and a patient teacher, with whom I have spent many intimate Sunday evenings . . . I know you very well and have even become familiar with your pattern of speech and can recognize your favorite phrases.[138]

British fans hardly ever admitted such feelings of intimacy with Clark. At the press conference held immediately after the medal ceremony at the National Gallery of Art Clark was initially reluctant to speculate as to why the American response was so much more powerful. 'Oh, I don't think I ought to answer that question,' he stated, 'I mean who am I to say anything about the American people?'

Under pressure, however, he did hazard an opinion:

> I think they felt – they always feel a need of something to hold on to. The American people have a great form of undirected or unsatisfied belief. People are not believing in me, but they wanted to believe in history. They wanted to believe they were part of an historical process. They wanted to believe that such a thing as a man could improve himself. That man had made his way through all kinds of troubles and got out on top. That they wanted to believe in.[139]

A doctor in a
time of plague

117

With political assassinations, Vietnam and riots in Los Angeles,
Newark and other cities, Americans needed all the comfort they
could get.

Meanwhile public television continued to enjoy a rocky
relationship with government, and was felt to have failed to reach an
audience outside a white, upper-middle-class, college-educated elite on
both coasts. *TV Guide* ran a cover story entitled 'Public Television:
Is Anybody Watching?' in August 1971, two months before *Civilisation*
was repeated on PBS. In it Richard K. Doan wrote

Funny thing happened to public TV, so called, on the way to . . . well,
wherever it was going: It became upper-class TV. Darling of TV's
disenchanted. Pet of TV's critics. All but ignored by TV's masses.
That's public TV. Nearly everybody (or so it seems) *talks* about public TV.
Boy, how they warm over *Sesame Street*, *The Forsyte Saga*, *Civilisation*,
The First Churchills and all that! But do many of them *watch* it? Not so you
can notice.[140]

President Nixon continued to insist that PBS decentralise, downsize and
stay out of current affairs. In June 1972 he vetoed a PBS funding bill.
He did it again in 1974, when Congress sent him a bill that would have
guaranteed funding for five years. 'Why, if our impact was so feeble, was
the White House so mad at us? ' asked Robert MacNeil (host of
NewsHour) bitterly in a piece for the *Washingtonian*, 'Where is public
television going?' Public television, he noted, was still internally riven
between localism and the desire to become a 'fourth network'. The latter
was the only real option, he argued. Public television had to broaden its
base by producing programmes 'along the broadest possible taste lines.
This still is consistent with the attempt to achieve excellence not only in
cultural programs like *Civilization*, but in light entertainment, music
and dance, drama, sports, and informational programming.'[141]
Although PBS survived a Congressional threat to 'zero-out' its budget in
1995 and has arguably superseded the BBC in news and current affairs,
a spate of often highly critical books suggests that it has otherwise failed
to resolve the dilemmas outlined here.[142]

118

6 Waiting for the Barbarians

I was brought up to believe that any work of art, music or literature that is enormously popular must have something seriously wrong with it. I see no reason why *Civilisation* should be an exception to this rule.[143]

Kenneth Clark, *The Other Half*

Clark did not expect *Civilisation* to last. 'I am quite certain that, in spite of the complimentary things you have said about the durability of the programmes', he wrote to Wheldon in June 1969,

> they will, in fact, be out of fashion in two or three years: not simply the moon shots and rockets, but the comments and even the small asides. They will sound as flat as successful comedy of the Thirties.[144]

In fact the popularity of the series, as we have seen, grew in the early 1970s. *Civilisation* was repeated in both the US and UK in 1971, reaching larger audiences than the original broadcast. BBC2 repeated it in 1972 and again in 1983, to mark Clark's death. In the United States the series would eventually break free from the PBS grip and migrate to cable. In late 1992, for example, it was shown on The Learning Channel (now known as TLC), part of an attempt by its new owner, the Discovery Channel, to liven up its staid image. In 2004 it was released on DVD by DD Home Entertainment. Amazon's UK site may set the parameters for its 'documentary' category pretty wide (it includes *Spooks* and *Top Gear*, for example), but *Civilisation* still makes the top 100.

'They don't make shows like *Civilisation* any more.' It's a sigh – of relief, in the case of some programme-makers. Is the series a somewhat quaint survivor from a past age, or does it still afford lessons for us today, forty years on? In a retrospect like this there is, as Clark foresaw, an inevitable tendency to present the series as a period-piece. Its production and reception history can smack of a period comedy of manners, notably in the generational divide between Clark and his critics. At the time of writing the print media are full of interviews of leading members of the '68 generation, few of them able or even willing to claim a legacy. In retrospect, therefore, Clark's fears for civilisation can seem exaggerated. Consensus remains on what the highlights of western art history are. Failures in the education system may mean that those under twenty are unfamiliar with them, but their elders for the most part agree on what they should know. There is a challenge or problem implicit in the much-touted mid-1990s survey which had Britons propose Rolf Harris as the most famous artist they knew. Though the notion of a canon was regularly ridiculed, in practice the 'new' art historians spent much of their time applying their new methodologies to the same works that 'old' art historians like Ernst Gombrich had wrestled with.

For the past forty years, therefore, there has been broad agreement on which historical figures and even which specific buildings, sculptures and paintings belong in art and history programmes. It becomes possible to pull back from the chronological approach adopted in earlier chapters and imagine something like a conversation between series made across the period, from *Civilisation* to Matthew Collings's *This Is Civilisation* (Channel 4, 2007). Deciding which series to include is an inexact science, but one can identify series that share a similar format: a clearly identified auteur leads the viewer on a personal journey over a series of episodes, using great works of art or architecture to inspire discussion of human creativity, society and progress.

, it is clear to me that Bronowski's
ıce in such a discussion, whereas
es not. The former speaks to
ter to the American experience.
ιe American view of their story as a
d world' history. As Gilan (Gill's
cleverness and rhythm', whereas
uth and love'.[145] Whereas
Malone found compelling locations
cure scientific theories come alive on
milar marriage of script and visuals.

...taking card payments into the future

streamline

As the crew was almost exactly the same as that on *Civilisation*, one has to assume that the fault lies with Cooke's failure to understand the difference between radio talks and television.

Civilisation established thirteen as the canonical number of episodes for such a series in the 1970s. Thirteen weeks fit into a quarter's

121

Pamela Tudor-Craig

programming. Since 1980, however, the number of episodes in a series has fallen. This process started with Robert Hughes's series on western art and architecture since 1880, *The Shock of the New* (BBC2, 1980), which had eight episodes. Pamela Tudor-Craig's *The Secret Life of Paintings* (BBC1, 1986) had five. *Secret Life* engaged special effects to travel across time and space in search of the secrets underlying familiar masterpieces. From the mid-1980s the format has settled at around half the number of episodes. Neil MacGregor's *Seeing Salvation* (1999) had four, Nigel Spivey's *How Art Made the World* (BBC2, 2005) five, and Collings's *Matt's Old Masters* (Channel 4, 2003) and *This Is Civilisation* four each. *Simon Schama's Power of Art* (BBC2, 2006) is a notable exception, with eight. Otherwise the only one to buck this trend has been Sister Wendy Beckett, a South African-born nun who made her television début in 1992, aged sixty-two. *Sister Wendy's Odyssey* (BBC2, 1992) consisted of seven ten-minute shorts, but she then fronted two series of ten hour-long episodes: *Sister Wendy's Grand Tour* (BBC2, 1994) and *Sister Wendy's Story of Painting* (BBC1, 1996). A final six half-hour programmes were produced by WGBH Boston in 2001, before Beckett returned to a life of contemplation. In addition to bucking the trend to shrink art series Beckett also pulled off the now unthinkable feat of getting an art series broadcast on BBC1, rather than BBC2, which has in turn passed the culture torch to television's 'Third Programme', BBC4.

In discussing these series in the context of *Civilisation*, therefore, we need to be aware of the greater demands imposed by the BBC and Channel 4 on directors and presenters. With fewer episodes in which to establish a rhythm and style of their own, they have been obliged to borrow techniques from a range of other formats. Period dress, scientific experiments and a focus on the machinery of research itself have all been used to create a sense of the journey unfolding in 'real time', rather than allowing the ideas to carry the viewer, as Montagnon put it. It is nonetheless still possible to identify enough common ground across four decades of programming for the proposed 'conversation' between these series to be possible. Three topics seem particularly promising. First is the presenter and their mode of address. What conditions have to apply for the charge of being patronising to stick? As we have seen, this is a familiar debate to have around *Civilisation*. The next two issues are less frequently raised, if more important. We have the question of how to portray the artist's relationship with society. Is it possible to imagine a programme on art that would *not* interpret works as windows on a troubled renegade who 'breaks all the rules'?

Finally we have the question of art's place in a universal human experience. From John Berger through Robert Hughes and up to Simon Schama there has been a trend towards portraying art as a symptom of malaise, in both the medical sense, but also in the sense of *malaise*, a perennial state of being uneasy, haunted, watchful. In Berger's case, it is a socio-political malaise, in Schama's it is individuated as a case study. Art has considerable political or psychological power. This power is 'masked' or 'coded', and so television series about art become dramas in which a presenter unveils that power for us, without rendering it accessible. Art has a bloom, but it is peaky, unhealthy. Although *Civilisation* certainly admitted that creativity could become overblown, it saw art as the result of a natural and healthy process, as a function of being more truly alive. Though they prefer to speak of becoming more

123

Simon Schama

'truly human' rather than more 'alive', otherwise Bronowski, Nigel Spivey and Matthew Collings seem to adopt a similarly positive and accessible approach.

Patronise Me

Clark repeatedly made the point that the risks of aiming too high were less than those of pandering. 'The majority of people, although not well informed, are surprisingly receptive and like to have their minds stretched. They would much rather miss an obscure allusion than feel they were being talked down to.'[146]

And the evidence of fan mail and of American critics in particular suggests that viewers actually found it gratifying to miss the odd allusion. Rather than feeling patronised, it was pleasant to be in the company of a presenter who was confident of the viewer's, as well as his own interest. As *TV Guide*'s Cleveland Amory put it, Clark 'presumes so much. He actually overrates us – and the effect is exhilarating.'[147]

To level the charge of being patronising is tantamount to adopting the role of guardian *vis-à-vis* a third person, who is presumed to be unable to defend themselves. 'Don't patronise me' is not a command or threat. By saying it we reveal that we are not in fact the ignorant individual our interlocutor considers us to be. Strictly speaking it is not possible to patronise anyone. Although we can experience being patronised vicariously, to adopt the angelic guise and endeavour to defend others from a danger they will not perceive themselves is, well, highly patronising. To accuse a presenter of talking down does not challenge or question the existence of a hierarchy of cultural capital, it simply asserts our claim to be able to read off a specific audience's degree of comprehension more accurately than the presenter's fumbling efforts.

The question of whether or not a given programme is patronising reflects programme-makers' and television executives' beliefs that they know their audiences better than the audiences do themselves, and so are already positioned to provide suitable fare. There was an arrogance in the Reithian mission to give audiences programming that was 'good for them'. How different is that arrogance which vows to give audiences programming that is 'suitable for their age, education and class'? It is striking that our faith in such metrics seems to be proof against the suspicions we now have of them when deployed in the context of politics, where we know how much survey data is influenced by the way the question is posed. Other, equally anachronistic presuppositions inform the way in which presenters introduce their topic to the audience. We have seen how much arts programming in both the US and UK has come with a pre-emptive warning that what we are about to see contains no history or art whatsoever, that this new series has passion, fighting, rebels and blood – the stuff we 'get'. Such a warning launched Clark's *Is Art Necessary?* in 1958. In the US it appeared in a somewhat less forbidding guise on ABC's *Omnibus*, where Alistair Cooke was always ready with a suave anecdote that reassured us that the next bit of culture wouldn't hurt a bit. Such self-denial is now unnecessary. So are the jibes at academe that so often accompanied them. Art history may have seemed an over-theorised Germanic import in the late 19th century, but it hardly represents an ogre today, unless we make it so. In many cases, including Clark's own, the apologies can seem self-serving and insincere. They smack of cod heroics. The academic has struck upon the new-found land of television, and has to burn his boats to keep warm. It is time to lose the fiction that everyone is put off by art or history, and that academe and the media are mutually exclusive career paths.

125

Producing television about Old Masters while promising the viewer something entirely different is bound to be something of a magic act, calling for plenty of smoke and mirrors. Pamela Tudor-Craig's 1986 series *The Secret Life of Paintings* series shows how mystery can totally overwhelm the art it supposedly surrounds. Produced by Dick Foster, each episode focuses on one painting, such as Uccello's *St George and the Dragon*, and sees the presenter explore its iconography, using special effects, techno-synthesizer chords and a lavishly dressed set that is a necromancer's dream. Paintings appear as reluctant, uncooperative witnesses, yet Tudor-Craig reassures us that 'patient detective work and just a little imagination may still unlock their secrets'. 'Subconscious springs' bubble, 'waters of chaos' swirl, creating a mood that has been compared to a Hammer horror film.[148] The Uccello episode, for example, ends with the presenter linking the nuclear bomb with the painted dragon, highlighting today's need for 'a divine dragon slayer'. Torch-lit romps through museums at night, mysterious codes, hybrid cults, myths with messages for our own times. There was much in *Secret Life* that anticipates *The Da Vinci Code* (2004) and the celebrity cults of Scientology and kabbala. The success of Dan Brown's book and the subsequent film has in turn spawned rip-off documentaries such as Tony Robinson's *The Real Da Vinci Code* (Channel 4, 2006). Presenters appear with lamp in hand, exploring tombs and caves. The pilot episode of *How Art Made the World* features clips from the video game *Lara Croft, Tomb Raider*, and Spivey rarely lets go of the lamp, even when he is standing in Piccadilly Circus.

126

By focusing on mystery for its own sake, programme-makers solve the problem of identifying a subject, at the expense of the art they claim to decode. Rather than offering a more accessible alternative to the 'presenter as hero', these series suggest a 'presenter as magician' model. Clark's knowledge was lightly worn, and shared in a conversational tone. He was not a keeper of secrets. Truth had a glow of its own, rather than being something that lurked in the darkness, waiting to be stumbled upon. In his journey Clark did come across objects or cultures that were poorly understood, where scholars and others disagreed over interpretation. Rather than posing as expert, Clark was as likely to shrug his shoulders and move on. Although I've noted the travelogue element in *Civilisation*, in both the programmes and in the surrounding publicity there was no sense of the series as a 'search for' civilisation, as a pursuit of a fugitive mystery. Places were visited for their own sake, as agents of civilisation, rather than illustrations.

In the 1970s we see a shift in how presenters used locations. In Bronowski's *Ascent* and Hughes's *Shock of the New*, the presenter

Bronowski

takes us to a place to illustrate a particular point about his subject.
The 'magic carpet' approach travels too erratically for there to be a
sense of a journey in pursuit of answers. The presenter already has the
answers before he sets out, and so appears all the more authoritative.
Bronowski, not Clark, is the epitome of the 'presenter as hero', even if
his style of delivery is idiosyncratic. No Autocue for him. Bronowski
squeezes out his lines as if thinking them out on the spot. He repeatedly
interrupts his already slow delivery for pauses, as he racks his brain for
exactly the right word. Although it seems unscripted, in shot after shot
Bronowski's progress through a particular location is actually very slick,

with particular views, objects or artefacts coming into vision just as the presenter requires them. The viewer is enthralled. The more one watches the more one is overwhelmed by Bronowski's brilliance. There are limits, indeed, to how far one can compare *Ascent* with other programmes; Bronowski is a genius, whereas Clark and his successors are not. Rather than being alienated by this superiority, respect for his mind has the effect of making us almost solicitous towards him as a human being. We strain expectantly for every word, each of which seems a little victory over barriers, a vault over disciplinary boundaries, as well as those between present and past, between intelligence and language itself (despite his perfect English, one can tell it is not his first language).

It might seem odd to discuss *The Ascent of Man* alongside *Civilisation*. But as Attenborough has noted, the series was 'an affirmation about mankind', an affirmation of a process – 'scientific probing' – 'which is a paramount quality in civilisation. Oddly. Science is central, and although it wasn't called *Civilisation*, it's also about civilisation.'[149] And a psychological or palaeontological approach to art as a creation of an evolved mind has recently been revived. In the last ten years some art-history documentaries have started to mimic science documentaries. Nigel Spivey's *How Art Made the World* is constructed along the lines of a *Horizon* science documentary of the 1990s, with a pinch of *CSI* (CBS, 2000–) thrown in. In the first episode we meet a scientist, who talks while silhouetted in front of a projected slide image (a classic *Horizon* shot) of a work of art. First-person narrative stresses the presenter's journey to several sites in the search for answers to questions about human visual perception. We literally look over his shoulder as he works in libraries and see him wandering through the library stacks (another well-worn visual).

In the words of director Mark Hedgecoe, *How Art Made the World* aims to show 'that art is an intrinsic human activity,' to bring home 'the importance of imagery'.[150] Each episode sees Spivey explain contemporary uses and abuses of art by referring back to the supposed discovery on the part of unindividuated prehistoric artists of universal

128

Science as art's alibi: Nigel Spivey

truths regarding human perception. These discoveries are then tested
using an array of contemporary gadgets and psychological
experiments on university students and, in one episode, gull chicks.
Art-historical development is flattened by psychological constants.
Indeed, so strong is the urge to enlist science to explain the artistic
impulse that individual expression, agency or choice almost threatens
to disappear. Humans are, it suggests, captives of their brain's peculiar
circuitry.

129

  We are, Spivey reveals, programmed to find certain shapes
beautiful. Science comes close to trumping aesthetics. Spivey hesitates
before pronouncing two Greek bronzes to be 'the greatest works of
sculpture in the world', and avoids looking at the camera when he does
so. Recognition of beauty is a private 'moment', a weakness yet to be
excused or explained away as a (mis?)function of our brains, rather than
as a recognition of a universal truth. There are many ways in which an
over-engineered take on art history is nonetheless preferable to the
'renegade artist' trope that I shall consider next. Though the lab can
seem as remote as the art museum, the authority of science can carry us
a long way.

Rebels without Cause

In their haste to demonstrate that they are not about the history of art, documentaries have also become histories of troubled artists that 'play against type', against our expectations of how an Old Master should behave. Of course, the troubled genius has been a trope since the late 18th century at least. One wonders that it can still surprise us to discover that artists are sometimes nonconformists. Playing artists against type is even more problematic today, however, in so far as it assumes a certain amount of prior knowledge on the part of the viewer. *Simon Schama's Power of Art* repeatedly promises to introduce us to Mr Hyde, assuming that we've already met Dr Jekyll. We are not going to see *that* artist, the dull one; we will see a different artist: not 'our Turner', 'our Van Gogh', but 'the Turner you don't know', 'the other Van Gogh'. I suspect that those interested in learning more about art may well feel excluded, or simply confused: 'Who's Van Gogh?' might be the question on their lips, rather than 'Whose?' Meanwhile, those who *do* have an image of Turner are irritated by a presenter who is literally promising to tell us something we don't know.

130

He can paint, too

Artist rebels demand costumed actors and the reconstruction of paintings through tableaux vivants. In an interview about the making of *Simon Schama's Power of Art*, Schama recalls how he and his producer, Clare Bevan agreed at the start that they would avoid the 'men in stick-on beards' approach, but also be careful not to be 'too flashy, not to pretend you're Hollywood'. Episode 1 opens with a costumed actor alone, as Caravaggio, struggling along a beach, then waving a sword, then a dagger at the camera, then running. Twenty details from his paintings flash by in a few seconds, then we have the title credits, which show blood dripping into clear liquid. Later the actor bursts into a tavern, where a party of drinkers reacts, creating a tableau vivant that recalls a Caravaggio painting shown immediately afterwards. Swords are waved in almost every episode, in fact, including the one on Rothko. The series experiments slightly: in some the camera and a third-party narrator adopt a 'fly-on-the-wall' perspective, with Caravaggio filmed *contre-jour*; costumed artists sometimes speak directly to a camera, sometimes they do not. In 'Van Gogh' there is even a clever attempt to suggest interaction between the painter and Schama as presenter. In the Rothko episode the presenter is doubled, with 'Young Simon' shown in a soft-focus sequence that has been distressed to look like it is filmed on Super-8.

The use of costume began in the mid-1960s in documentaries by Ken Russell and Leslie Megahey. As early as 1970 this approach had become something of a cliché, with Gill writing of documentaries 'in which costumed actors pranced and capered in the mid-distance, backlit, across fields'.[151] An economical sort of visual shorthand was used to show the artist in different moods, with poses held for quite long periods of time. From around the time of Alan Yentob's *Leonardo* (2003) onwards actors and reconstruction have been employed in much more cinematic ways. As Wyver has observed, opening sequences seethe with panting violence, serving 'to bludgeon a viewer into paying attention'.[152]

Otherwise the rebel approach is little changed from that which the *Burlington Magazine* critiqued in 1974:

131

What haunt the producers of all television programmes are fears that
viewers will either switch off or switch over to another channel. Hence the
need to cultivate the effective, the immediate: anything so long as people
go on watching. And so, through the hoops, the artists are made to go.
Cézanne has to be 'the savage genius'; Leighton becomes the 'grand Vizier
of Victorian painting', not to mention an 'Olympian zombie'. El Greco's
paintings have to 'defy all the laws of composition and colour'. . . . It is
rarely a case of bringing the People to Cézanne on Cézanne's terms; usually
a matter of presenting Cézanne to the People on the People's terms . . . .
Most producers tend to assume, and they are probably correct, that the
general public are not actually very interested in works of art as such,
preferring to see and be told about the success stories, the eccentricities,
the financial value and the sex appeal that surround artists and what they
create. A feeling that the pill must be sugared accounts for the emphasis,
wherever possible, on personality, reconstruction and location shooting . . . .
Hence, too, the often disastrous fondness for tableaux vivants [that] . . .
encourage one of the most popular fallacies about the visual arts: that the
artist depicts exactly what he sees.[153]

Such a passage should give us pause before seeing the 1970s as a golden
age of the authored documentary series. Great series like *Civilisation*
were not produced in a prelapsarian age of innocence. Directors and
presenters faced similar challenges. They simply chose to respond
differently back then.

Of course, a focus on mystery or artist-rebels also has an
impact on the presenter's relationship to the viewer. To offer a diagnosis
of art is to present oneself as an expert diagnostician. To read the runes
of artistic mysteries is to be a shaman or magician. Whether they elicit
respect or wonder, both roles establish a clear distance between
presenter and viewer. Though they may unmask the artist's 'real
nature', by interpreting it as a revolt against social norms they do little
to render artists or their work more approachable. And here we come to
a crucial point. The logic behind the 'renegade' trope is simple, if tragic:
the more we present Old Masters in terms of revolution, social

dislocation and the failure of artist and public to engage, the more 'modern' they become. This art work was, we are breathlessly informed, as controversial to its time as Tracey Emin's unmade bed is to ours. That is, it would seem, the best way we have to make old art appear significant.

Though it is a comfort of sorts to dress up the unique dysfunctions of contemporary art in period dress, much is lost if we suggest that great art is *sui generis* shocking as well as sick. Art becomes a captive of politics. Admittedly, this prison can seem rather exciting, even extensive; there is a politics of gender, race and class to be explored. Gilan recalls how 'young people, we were all into *Ways of Seeing*, it was our politics, it was everything that we were doing. Everything was political . . . . It was all about the now.'[154] It can seem that all art is politics, and all politics is art, an exercise in trying not to get screwed. But that isn't enough if we want to speak to a public as human beings, and point to how creativity is innate, universal, healthy and pre-political, how great art has made and can make us better people. In presenting the development of art on television, programme-makers have a choice to make: to be wise, or wised up. *Civilisation* is ultimately an illustration of Duke of Urbino Federigo da Montefeltro's motto: *essere humano* ('be human').

133

Being Human

Directed by Michael Dibb, Berger's *Ways of Seeing* (1970) is a brilliant rejoinder to *Civilisation*, a 'television argument' full of arresting contrasts and beautifully cut sequences. 'They were complementary to one another: two sides of a coin,' Montagnon observes, 'I hesitate to say which is the obverse, and which is the real side.'[155] There are several digs at Clark and the art-historical establishment (which Berger tends to lump together) for being obscurantist and nostalgic toadies to an inegalitarian culture that is, happily, in decline. Yet Berger can seem unable to imagine how

Berger slashes a
Botticelli in *Ways
of Seeing*

creativity can continue. Now that artists and viewers have eaten of
the tree and perceived the extent to which all images are abused, what
hope remains? There is no solace in the Old Masters for Berger, a man
who can dismiss all painting in oils as glorifying the capitalist ability
'to buy, furnish and to own'. Nothing if not consistent, Berger refuses
to exempt his own commentary from this. 'You receive meanings that
I arrange,' he warns, advising us to be sceptical. He weighs the world
of art and finds it wanting, even as he concedes that there is no solid
ground under his feet.

Though broadcast fourteen years later, Robert Hughes's *The
Shock of the New* was still struggling to escape this tragic state. In
episode 3, Hughes bemoans modernism's lack of values, citing how
effectively it could be appropriated by Communist, capitalist or fascist
regimes, without there being a sense of abuse or misappropriation.
Standing among the soulless towers of Albany's Empire State Plaza
(Wallace K. Harrison and Max Abramovitz, 1965–79) Hughes remarks
on how little difference it makes whether one imagines a swastika,
Communist star or corporate logo placed on top. In a century marked
by genocide and industrialised war, he says, one cannot think of a single
work of art of which it could be said 'this work made men more just to
one another', or 'this saved a single Jew or Vietnamese'. Although

Robert Hughes

Hughes's permanent squint, scowl and occasionally drawled delivery make him a somewhat cold presenter, otherwise *Shock* is happy to celebrate modernism as a bunch of revolutionaries liberating us from the Old Master tradition.

Shock opens with a globe-trotting sequence in which Hughes makes the usual promise that this is not going to be a history of modern art. Instead he wishes to show how modern art

> has acted upon society and vice versa, how it has dealt, for instance, with the idea of pleasure, how it has tried to confirm or reject the political status quo, how it has tried to construct utopias, and so on.

'We are at the end of the modern period,' he continues, 'and art no longer acts on us like it did on our grandfathers. I want to find out why.' Produced by Lorna Pegram, *Shock* proceeds through the period chronologically, and devotes considerable effort to creating sequences of stills and special effects that recreate the look of Cubism, Futurism and other styles, in a particularly insistent development of the tableau vivant noted above. Hughes evinces very little enthusiasm or affection for his subjects. Although he notes that modernism is now over, he does not appear to mourn its passing, nor see any grounds for hope that something better might follow in its wake.

As we have seen, some critics felt that, though warmer and affectionate, *Civilisation* was also a farewell, a closing of the museum door to the possibility of any future art. Throughout this book I've drawn attention to the pessimistic lens through which Clark viewed the achievements of western civilisation. But *Civilisation*'s stature as a work of art in itself enables it to escape Clark's pessimism, in the same way that every work of art has a life independent of its creator. The documentaries of Berger, Hughes and Schama are powerful and carefully edited, but in a self-consciously clever fashion. They are a collection of quotations and conceits that sometimes descends into shorthand. The images and meanings are elsewhere. The director and presenter 'arrange' them in a sort of bricolage. Though the result is undoubtedly fast-paced, it assumes a large amount of prior knowledge in the process, at least if we are to pick up on all the works that are being borrowed. Gill and his colleagues did not assume a large amount of prior knowledge, that we had 'seen it all before'. They saw their role as much more than arranger of somebody else's meaning. The images and meanings are in the film itself, in the use of rostrum camerawork, location filming and in the editing itself.

As Wyver notes, *Civilisation* had 'textures of an original artwork lovingly filmed, but also textures of thought alluded to by the poetic achievement of filmmaking'.[156] Although they had foresworn the sort of fashionable 'fancy work' that might have earned them professional accolades (there were no BAFTAs, bar one for the editor, Allan Tyrer), their programmes had a richness that defied the medium's supposed obsession with immediacy, with surface. Crittenden sympathises with those who argue that film can never communicate with, only speak at the viewer.

136

You only see a surface which is supposed to represent some kind of human experience, but which actually doesn't involve us. We need to learn how to reengage the audience. All old art becomes less relevant to us, because we are not engaging with it directly. Film can seem to close the viewer off. There is a barrier – such as never existed in the best of theatre. In that separation it seems you can attempt anything, can misrepresent. We ought to be skeptical about its value, therefore, but it doesn't mean that we shouldn't find an innate beauty and value in the best art of all ages, something which should be celebrated.[157]

Happily, there are programmes that have been willing to acknowledge 'innate beauty and value', even if they do so allusively, even if the words themselves remain off limits, along with 'civilisation' itself.

Neil MacGregor and Sister Wendy Beckett have played a key role in reintroducing the idea of great art as something that speaks to universal human emotions. Greatness can be something that connects us to masterpieces, rather than cutting us off from them. With a greater focus on the thoughts and emotions of the figures represented in the paintings, the figure of the painter has been gently nudged to one side. The paintings are not seen as depicting 'the inside of the artist's head'. Whereas costumed reconstructions strive to achieve authenticity by quoting or paraphrasing diaries or other records, these programmes acknowledge a truth that should be obvious: that great painters are usually not great writers or talkers, that the 'drama' of their works is not dependent on how colourful a life they led themselves. MacGregor and Beckett evoke the writings of Walter Pater. Pater saw culture as reconnecting us with our best, most unified and balanced selves. The aim of engaging with art was the same as that of engaging with any other part of the world: to rouse us to a life of constant and eager observation. 'The chief use in studying old masters,' as opposed to more recent works, lies in the fact that artistic qualities and characteristics are, Pater says, 'written larger, and are easier to read [in them] than the analogues of them in all the mixed, confused productions of the modern mind.'[158] Pater saw old art as inspirational, not because of its survival,

137

good taste or historical significance, but because it picked out the passionate elements of a universal human nature. Clark was definitely an admirer, noting in his 1961 edition of Pater's *The Renaissance* that the latter overtakes 'in the candour and subtlety of his analysis, all the critics of his time and [draws] level with the ideas of our own day'.[159]

The first series to take on the 'c-word', Matthew Collings's *This Is Civilisation* visits many of the same places and works of art familiar from previous series: the Arena Chapel, David's 'The Death of Marat', etc. The atmosphere is relaxed, intimate, contemplative, somewhat minimalist. There are no attempts at costume or reconstruction, the music is 'chill-out room' loungecore and Collings's voice relatively quiet and uninflected. Although there is some gorgeous location photography, there is no sense of 'journey' or pursuit. When in vision Collings is usually in a gallery, shoulders hunched, pacing back and forth in front of a canvas like a caged animal, regularly looking away from the camera and apparently speaking off the cuff. The script is full of short sentences without being breathless, and regularly uses slang, again without a cheeky wink or any desire to shock. The tone is one of calm seriousness, and the presenter's lack of pretension enables him to say some things that would be highly patronising, were they delivered in a programme that followed the 'presenter as magician' model. 'Don't worry, I'll help you', Collings promises when we see David's *Oath of the Horatii*. There are some knowing asides, but not enough to grate. 'Silence in the court, while the ads are on,' Collings says (a Bergerian touch), just before the commercial break. The inevitably abbreviated background information is well delivered, and occasionally playful. 'He's radical, he's dark and he lives in Spain' may be a schematic description of Francisco Goya, but it certainly isn't overblown.

Nor is radical darkness the point. Collings is using the artworks to point to emotions he believes we have lost the ability to feel. 'We've forgotten what it is to be great.' Episode 3, 'Save Our Souls' sees him highlight the relevance of Ruskin to contemporary society's ills. We learn about Venice, the Pre-Raphaelite and Arts and Crafts movements. 'We don't know how to be serious,' Collings states, 'art can

Matthew Collings

show us.' It can also show us 'how to be civilised', though Collings
rarely uses the adjective or noun, and fights shy of defining either. He is
more outspoken in attacking the world of contemporary art, which, he
argues, encourages a superficial appreciation of art that fails to improve
us. It is astonishing to hear a presenter inviting us to be great, serious,
emotive human beings. Collings echoes Clark in noting that the words
alone appear ludicrous, they are not 'urgent terms' to us. Apart from the
sometimes tokenistic appearances of Brian Sewell, it is astonishing to
hear such criticism of the art world on television, not least on Channel 4,
whose coverage of the Turner Prize is piously iconoclastic. Like
Civilisation and *The Ascent of Man*, *This Is Civilisation* is about what
makes us human. It shows that there is an alternative to 'bludgeoning'
viewers, that a film about the Old Masters can say truly revolutionary
things if it has the restraint to resist the urge to dramatise.

'I don't think you should try too hard,' Montagnon observed
in an interview for this book. 'I think a more Zen approach to the whole
subject is called for.' MacMillan sees a failure of nerve in the trend to
import 'perky personalities' rather than trust in the abilities of a
genuinely charismatic presenter talking to camera. To them and their
fellow crew members, *Civilisation* was not a nostalgic farewell to artistic

139

Into the light

greatness but a way of reminding viewers of the possibilities. Although the idea of this set of individuals collaborating originally seemed unlikely, their creativity and enthusiasm tempered Clark's pessimism and hero-worship at the same time as it reinforced his awareness of the potential that lay in civilised places, textures and shapes. This creative dialogue can be seen in the rich, layered quality of the finished product, which has yet to be matched.

Like Clark himself, the crew were taken aback by the popularity of *Civilisation*, and occasionally puzzled at the earnest way in which it was read by Americans. In political terms it became a hostage to institutions such as the BBC and PBS, almost becoming a cipher for them in debates about television policy. To television makers, *Civilisation* is something imposed on them from without. It is striking that, in a sector where grandiloquence is not entirely unknown, *Civilisation*'s scale, confidence and ambition seem delusionary, almost offensive. To make eight centuries of human creativity understandable to an international audience with widely varying degrees of cultural capital. To take a risk with an unfamiliar and expensive new format, and pitch it at everyone. To a medium that appears all too quick to accept the neatly classified, shrink-wrapped audiences delivered by an explosion in channels, such actions must appear arrogant.

This book has circled around the questions *Civilisation* poses about human progress; its ironies, its risks and its potential rewards. It has also traced a smaller debate about the risks and rewards involved in using television to bring some of mankind's greatest achievements to as broad a public as possible. Both boil down to a question of faith, to holding one's nerve. Earlier on in this chapter I implied a dichotomy between being wise and being wised-up. The lesson of *Civilisation* is that we can be both.

Notes

Key to abbreviations:
BBC: BBC Written Archives Centre,
Caversham
NGA: National Gallery of Art Archives,
Washington
NPBA: National Public Broadcasting
Archives, University of Maryland, College
Park
TBA: Tate Archives, London

1 Sir David Attenborough, featurette
interview in *Civilisation* DVD set, 2004.
2 Kenneth Clark, *The Other Half*
(London: John Murray, 1977), p. 210.
3 Clark, *The Other Half*, pp. 222–3.
4 Barry Norman, 'Is This the New *Forsyte
Saga*?', unidentified clipping, BBC,
T53/325/1.
5 Cited in Peter Fiddick, 'A Gleam in the
Public Eye', *Guardian*, 2 February 1979.
6 Laurie Ouellette, *Viewers Like You?
How Public TV Failed the People* (New York:
Columbia University Press, 2002), p. 98.
7 John Wyver, *Vision On: Film, Television
and the Arts in Britain* (London: Wallflower,
2007), pp. 145–6.
8 John Walker, *Arts TV: A History of Arts
Television in Britain* (London: John Libbey,
1993), p. 81.
9 Richard Weight, *Patriots: National Identity
in Britain, 1940–2000* (Basingstoke:
Macmillan, 2002), p. 470.
10 Clark, *The Other Half*, p. 274.
11 Peter Montagnon, interview with the
author, 2008.
12 Unedited transcript of National Gallery of
Art press conference, 18 November 1970.
NGA, Series 2C1, Box 21.
13 Clark to Burton, n.d. TBA, 8812.1.4.90.

14 Michael Gill, *Growing into War*
(Stroud: Sutton, 2005), p. 274.
Compare Clark, *The Other Half*, p. 211.
15 Clark to Burton, 15 April 1967. TBA,
8812.1.4.90.
16 BBC, T49/72/1. Clark overlooks this
programme in his autobiography, claiming
that his only television appearance prior to
1958 was as chairman of a 1937 art-and-
poetry panel game. Clark, *The Other Half*,
p. 205.
17 Trustee Minutes, 13 April 1937.
National Gallery Archive, London.
18 From a lecture delivered at the Royal
Institution, n.d. [1942?]. TBA,
8812.2.2.309.
19 Kenneth Clark, 'Is Art Necessary in
Public?', n.d. [1944?]. TBA, 8812.2.2.46.
20 Bernard Sendall, *Independent Television
in Britain: Origin and Foundation,
1946–1962* (London: Macmillan, 1982),
p. 60.
21 Sir David Attenborough, featurette
interview in *Civilisation* DVD set, 2004.
22 Yvonne Gilan, interview with the author,
31 January 2008.
23 'Sir Kenneth Reaches the Peak', *Sunday
Observer*, 8 December 1963.
24 Bernard Sendall, *Independent Television
in Britain: Expansion and Change,
1958–1968* (London: Macmillan, 1983),
p. 93.
25 Clark, *The Other Half*, p. 207.
26 Norman Swallow, *Factual Television*
(London: Focal, 1966), p. 158.
27 Clark, *The Other Half*, p. 209.
28 Sendall, *Independent Television in
Britain: Origin and Foundation*, p. 351;
Kathleen Burk, *Troublemaker: The Life and*

History of A. J. P. Taylor (New Haven, CT: Yale University Press, 2000), p. 392.

29 Clark, *The Other Half*, p. 207.

30 Ken MacMillan, interview with the author, 17 January 2008.

31 Kenneth Clark, 'From the Few to the Many', 1966 Granada Lecture. Copy at TBA, 8812.2.2.326, f. 60.

32 Burk, *Troublemaker*.

33 Sendall, *Independent Television in Britain: Origin and Foundation*, pp. 164–82.

34 Sendall, *Independent Television in Britain: Origin and Foundation*, p. 113.

35 *Variety*, 18 January 1967.

36 TBA, 8812.2.1.11.

37 Michael Gill, 'Some Thoughts on Art Films' (unpublished essay, 1979), p. 18.

38 Gill, 'Some Thoughts on Art Films', pp. 12–13.

39 Roger Crittenden, interview with the author, 28 January 2008.

40 Burton to Clark, 28 November 1966. TBA, 8812.1.4.89.

41 For a flavour of his script, see the transcript of an earlier Home Service talk, 'Hellas Revisited', *Listener*, 22 January 1959, pp. 164–6.

42 Clark, *The Other Half*, p. 207.

43 Clark to Gill, 22 April 1967. TBA, 8812.1.4.90.

44 Clark, *The Other Half*, p. 213.

45 Raymond Williams, 'A Noble Past', *Listener*, 17 April 1969.

46 Gill to Clark, 31 December 1967. TBA, 8812.1.5.90.

47 Peter Montagnon, 'Notes for Meeting 17th May 1967' and Montagnon to Head of Arts Features, 21 June 1968. BBC, T53/177/1.

48 Clark to Rosamond M. Bettencourt, UCSF Medical Center, 31 December 1970. TBA, 8812.1.4.94a.

49 These notes are headed 'Danny Kaye Show'. The CBS series of that name ended in 1967, but Clark probably intended it as a

generic title for the various chat shows he was invited onto in the US. TBA, 8812.2.2.463.

50 Unedited transcript of National Gallery of Art press conference, 18 November 1970. NGA, Series 2C1, Box 21.

51 Catherine Porteous, interview with the author, 13 January 2008.

52 Roger Crittenden, interview with the author, 28 January 2008.

53 Gill, *Growing into War*, p. 285.

54 Kenneth Clark, 'Western Civilisation', n.d. TBA, 8812.1.4.90.

55 Clark, *The Other Half*, p. 222.

56 Gill, 'Some Thoughts on Art Films', p. 21.

57 Ken MacMillan, interview with the author, 17 January 2008.

58 Clive Bell, *Civilisation* (London: Penguin, 1928), p. 140.

59 TBA, 8812.2.1.11.

60 Clark, *Radio Times*, 8 December 1970.

61 Peter Montagnon, interview with the author, 20 January 2008.

62 Gill to Clark, 20 February 1967. TBA, 8812.1.5.90.

63 Clark to Gill, 25 February 1967. BBC, T53/175/1.

64 Catherine Porteous, interview with the author, 13 January 2008.

65 Clark, *The Other Half*, p. 217.

66 Clark to Gill, n.d. BBC, T53/175/1.

67 Peter Montagnon, interview with the author, 20 January 2008.

68 Clark to Gill, 14 March 1967. TBA, 8812.1.4.90.

69 Michael Gill, 'From *Civilisation* to *America*' (unpublished memoir, 1988–90), p. 5.

70 Gill, 'From *Civilisation* to *America*', p. 17.

71 Roger Crittenden, interview with the author, 28 January 2008.

72 Kenneth Clark, 'Civilisation', *Radio Times*, 8 December 1970.

73 Williams, 'A Noble Past'.

74 Gill to Montagnon, 3 August 1967, BBC, T53/169/1.

75 Quotes from Clark's first set of notes, the red notebook. TBA, 8812.2.1.11.

76 Peter Montagnon, interview with the author, 20 January 2008.

77 Gill, 'From *Civilisation* to *America*', pp. 22–3.

78 Roger Crittenden, interview with the author, 28 January 2008.

79 Clark, *The Other Half*, p. 222.

80 Wheldon to Clark, 29 November 1968. TBA, 8812.1.4.89.

81 Clark, *The Other Half*, p. 208.

82 BBC Audience Research Department, 2 May 1969. BBC, R9/7/99.

83 Gill, 'Some Thoughts on Art Films', pp. 10, 8.

84 Gill to Clark, 20 February 1967. TBA, 8812.1.4.90.

85 Clark, 'Civilisation', Ep. 1 draft, n.d. BBC, T53/175/1.

86 Eleanor van Zandt, 'The Making of *Civilisation*', *Scholastic Voice*, 19 October 1970, p. 3.

87 Donald Hopson to Clark, 25 July 1972. TBA, 8812.1.4.91.

88 TBA, 8812.2.1.11.

89 TBA, 8812.2.2.1087.

90 Clark to Otto F. Schlaak, n.d. TBA, 8812.1.4.92.

91 Clark, 'From the Few to the Many', ff. 67–8.

92 Peter Montagnon, interview with the author, 20 January 2008.

93 John Sparrow, 'Civilisation', *Listener*, 8 May 1969.

94 Stefan Collini, *English Pasts: Essays in History and Culture* (Oxford: Oxford University Press, 1999), p. 263.

95 Raymond Williams, *Television: Technology and Cultural Form*, ed. Ederyn Williams (London: Routledge, 2003), p. 37.

96 Raymond Williams, 'Personal Relief Time', *Listener*, 20 March 1969, p. 399.

97 Clark, 'Civilisation', *Radio Times*.

98 Williams, *Television*, p. 93.

99 Williams, 'A Noble Past'.

100 Collini, *English Pasts*, p. 216.

101 John Berger, *Ways of Seeing* (London: Penguin, 1972), pp. 23, 29.

102 Berger, *Ways of Seeing*, p. 32.

103 Walker, *Arts TV*, p. 99.

104 John Russell, '*Civilisation*', *New York Times Book Review*, 26 April 1970.

105 Giles Waterfield, interview with the author, 16 January 2008.

106 'Clark on Civilisation', *Burlington Magazine* no. 111, June 1969, pp. 331–2 (331).

107 F. J. B. Watson, 'Sir Kenneth Clark', *Burlington Magazine* no. 125, November 1983, pp. 690–1 (690).

108 Ken MacMillan, interview with the author, 17 January 2008.

109 TBA, 8812.1.4.88.

110 Unedited transcript of National Gallery of Art press conference, 18 November 1970. NGA, Series 2C1, Box 21.

111 Patrick Wright, *On Living in an Old Country* (London: Verso, 1985).

112 *National Observer*, 22 December 1969.

113 Carter Brown to Clark, 18 September 1970. TBA, 8812.1.4.92.

114 Carter Brown to Clark, 18 September 1970. TBA, 8812.1.4.92.

115 Kennedy to Carter Brown, 14 October 1970. NGA, 'Civilisation Film Series – State Department and Senate', Series 2C1, J. Carter Brown Office Files, Box 21.

116 Clark, *The Other Half*, p. 225.

117 Gill, 'From *Civilisation* to *America*', p. 24.

118 John J. Dietsch, 'Television's Brainy Superstar', *Miami Herald*, 6 December 1970.

119 Clark to Carter Brown, 23 November 1970. NGA, Series 2C1, Box 21.

120 Clark, *The Other Half*, p. 244.

121 Clark to Carter Brown, 8 December 1970. NGA, Series 2C1, Box 21.

122 Clark, *Civilisation*, *Radio Times*, 8 December 1970. 8812.1.4.88.

123 Mrs A. William Rosow (East Orange, NJ) to Clark, 11 December 1969. TBA, 8812.1.4.91.

124 BBC, R44/767/1 (booklet), R78/1,923/1 (sales).

125 *Xerox World*, 25 September 1970. NPBA, '*Civilisation* – Generic', WNET Programme File.

126 *TV Guide*, 20 February 1970, p. 25.

127 Human Resources Network, *Corporate Social Responsibility: Profiles of Involvement* (Radnor, PA: Chilton Book Co., 1974), pp. 229–33, 263–4, 298–300, 366–7, 368 (*Sesame Street*), 369, 395–6, 416, 438.

128 Frank Judge, 'A Special TV Night', *Detroit News*, 9 September 1970.

129 Alistair Cooke, 'A Famed British Correspondent Introduces You to *Civilisation*', *TV Guide*, 3 October 1970, pp. 20–3.

130 Sir David Attenborough, interview in *Civilisation* DVD featurette, 2004.

131 '*Civilisation*'. WNET Programme Files, NPBA.

132 WMVS, 'You and *Civilisation*', TBA, 8812.1.4.88.

133 Jack Gould, 'TV: Civilisation and Home Screen Are Well Met', *New York Times*, 8 October 1970.

134 WMVS, 'You and *Civilisation*'.

135 'College Credit for "*Civilisation*"', *Xerox World*, 30 October 1970, p. 3.

136 Patti and Harry Brown to Clark, n.d. [December 1970]. TBA, 8812.1.4.91.

137 Anna Lee and Bob Colp (New York), to Clark, 8 December 1970. TBA, 8812.1.4.94a.

138 Doris Altier to Clark, 11 November 1971 and 12 April 1972. TBA, 8812.1.4.97c.

139 Unedited transcript of National Gallery of Art press conference, 18 November 1970. NGA, Series 2C1, Box 21.

140 Richard K. Doan, 'Public Television: Is Anybody Watching?', *TV Guide*, 21 August 1971, pp. 5–7 (5).

141 Robert MacNeil, 'Is Anybody Watching?', *Washingtonian*, October 1973.

142 Laurence Jarvik, *PBS: Behind the Screen* (Rocklin, CA: Prima, 1997); David Stewart, *The PBS Companion: A History of Public Television* (New York: TV Books, 1999); Ouellette, *Viewers Like You?*.

143 Clark, *The Other Half*, p. 226.

144 Clark to Wheldon, 4 June 1969. TBA, 8812.1.4.89.

145 Yvonne Gilan, interview with the author, 31 January 2008.

146 Clark, 'From the Few to the Many', f. 60.

147 Cleveland Amory, '*Civilisation*', *TV Guide*, 12 December 1970, p. 7.

148 Walker, *Arts TV*, p. 153.

149 Sir David Attenborough, interview in *Civilisation* DVD featurette, 2004.

150 Mark Hedgecoe, interview in DVD featurette, *How Art Made the World*.

151 Gill, 'Some Thoughts on Art Films', p. 20.

152 Wyver, *Vision On*, p. 157.

153 'Art on Television', *Burlington Magazine* no. 116, July 1974, pp. 365–6.

154 Yvonne Gilan, interview with the author, 31 January 2008.

155 Peter Montagnon, interview with the author, 20 January 2008.

156 Wyver, *Vision On*, p. 200.

157 Roger Crittenden, interview with the author, 28 January 2008.

158 Walter Pater, *The Renaissance* (London: Macmillan, 1910), p. 80.

159 Introduction to the Fontana Library edition of Walter Pater, *The Renaissance*, ed. Kenneth Clark (London: Fontana, 1961), p. 21.

Bibliography

Attenborough, David, *Life on Air: Memoirs of a Broadcaster* (London: BBC, 2002).

Attenborough, David, 'The Making of *Civilisation*', Special Feature on *Civilisation* DVD (2004).

Bell, Clive, *Civilisation* (London: Penguin, 1928).

Berger, John, *Ways of Seeing* (London: Penguin, 1972).

Bernstein, Marcelle, 'How Sir Kenneth Clark Distilled Civilisation into 13 Weekly Parts', *Observer*, 30 March 1969.

Black, Peter, 'Did Sir Kenneth Rivet You Too?', *Daily Mail*, 19 May 1969.

Briggs, Asa, *The BBC: The First Fifty Years* (Oxford: Oxford University Press, 1985).

Clark, Colette, Interview with the author, 27 January 2008.

Clark, Kenneth, 'From the Few to the Many', 1966 Granada Lecture. Copy at TBA, 8812.2.2.326, f. 60.

Clark, Kenneth, *Civilisation* (London: John Murray, 1969).

Clark, Kenneth, Interview with Joan Bakewell, *Listener*, 17 April 1969.

Clark, Kenneth, 'Civilisation', *Radio Times*, 8 December 1970.

Clark, Kenneth, *The Other Half* (London: John Murray, 1977).

Collini, Stefan, *English Pasts: Essays in History and Culture* (Oxford: Oxford University Press, 1999).

Cooke, Alistair, 'A Famed British Correspondent Introduces You to *Civilisation* and the Remarkable Lord Clark', *TV Guide*, 3 October 1970.

Corner, John (ed.), *Documentary and the Mass Media* (London: Edward Arnold, 1986).

Crittenden, Roger, Interview with the author, 28 January 2008.

Gilan, Yvonne, Interview with the author, 31 January 2008.

Gill, Michael, 'Some Thoughts on Art Films' (unpublished essay, 1979).

Gill, Michael, 'From *Civilisation* to *America*' (unpublished memoir, 1988–90).

Gill, Michael, *Growing into War* (Stroud: Sutton, 2005).

Gould, Jack, 'A Masterful Series on the Rise of Western Man', *New York Times*, 10 September 1970.

Hilmes, Michele (ed.), *The Television History Book* (London: BFI, 2003).

Jarvik, Laurence, *PBS: Behind the Screen* (Rocklin, CA: Prima, 1997).

Last, Richard, 'A Stupendous Triumph in the Making', *Sun*, 24 February 1969.

Last, Richard, 'Sir Kenneth's Magnificent Human Saga', *Sun*, 19 May 1969.

MacMillan, Ken, Interview with the author, 17 January 2008.

Montagnon, Peter, Interview with Norman Swallow, (BECTU History Project), 31 October 1995.

Montagnon, Peter, Interview with the author, 20 January 2008.

Ouellette, Laurie, *Viewers Like You? How Public TV Failed the People* (New York: Columbia University Press, 2002).

Porteous, Catherine, Interview with the author, 13 January 2008.

Priestley, J. B., 'Civilisation', *Sunday Times*, 25 May 1969.

Russell, John, '*Civilisation*', *New York Times Book Review*, 26 April 1970.

Secrest, Meryle, *Kenneth Clark: A Biography* (London: Weidenfeld and Nicolson, 1984).

Sendall, Bernard, *Independent Television in Britain: Origin and Foundation, 1946–1962* (London: Macmillan, 1982).

Sendall, Bernard, *Independent Television in Britain: Expansion and Change, 1958–1968* (London: Macmillan, 1983).

Stewart, David, *The PBS Companion: A History of Public Television* (New York: TV Books, 1999).

Sutton, Denys, Editorial, *Apollo*, April 1969.

Swallow, Norman, *Factual Television* (London: Focal, 1966).

Turner, Ann, Interview with the author, 12 January 2008.

Walker, John, *Arts TV: A History of Arts Television in Britain* (London: John Libbey, 1993).

Waterfield, Giles, Interview with the author, 16 January 2008.

Weight, Richard, *Patriots: National Identity in Britain, 1940–2000* (Basingstoke: Macmillan, 2002).

Williams, Raymond, 'Personal Relief Time', *Listener*, 20 March 1969.

Williams, Raymond, 'A Noble Past', *Listener*, 17 April 1969.

Williams, Raymond, *Television: Technology and Cultural Form*, ed. Ederyn Williams (London: Routledge, 2003).

Wyver, John, *Vision On: Film, Television and the Arts in Britain* (London: Wallflower, 2007).

Credits

Civilisation

United Kingdom/1969
BBC

directed by
Michael Gill
Peter Montagnon
Ann Turner
produced by
Michael Gill
Peter Montagnon
assistant producer
Ann Turner
lighting cameraman
A. A. Englander FRPS
camera
Kenneth MacMillan
second unit camera
Jimmy Court
supervising film editor
Allan Tyrer
editors
Roger Crittenden
Peter Heelas
Jesse Palmer
Michael Shah Dayan
chief assistant editor
Rosina Pedrick
sound
Basil Harris
Malcolm Webberley
Alan Dykes
Stanley Morcom
Dave Simpson
Peter Edwards
grip
Bill Paget
camera assistants
Adrian Coddington
Colin Deehan
Brian Easton
Tony Mayne
lighting
Jack Probert
Dave Griffiths
J. Cooksey
J. Taylor
J. Walker

148

research
June Leech
Christine Whitehead
production assistant
David Heycock
producers' assistants
Carol Jones
Maggie Houston
Elizabeth Baron
design
Tony Cornell
graphics
John Aston
stills direction
Ann Turner
stills photography
Roynon Raikes
Hugh Tosh
stills filming
Phil Summers
original music
Edwin Astley

© BBC

episode summaries

1. The Skin of Our Teeth
directed by Michael Gill
tx 23 February 1969

Clark begins in Paris, noting how the seemingly indestructible Roman civilisation collapsed, and how any and every civilisation must constantly face up to its enemies. He follows monks and itinerant craftsmen to the hostile reaches of Ireland's Atlantic coast, and contrasts Gaelic book illumination with Viking art. Charlemagne's reign brings this 'one prolonged Western' of the 7th and 8th centuries to a close. Political consolidation enables new experiments in art such as the Gero Cross.

2. The Great Thaw
directed by Peter Montagnon
tx 2 March 1969

The 12th century represents one of those periods in human history where man makes a great leap forward, 'an intensification of existence'. Exploring the abbeys and churches of Cluny, Moissac, Vezelay and Chartres, Clark finds manifestations of this irrepressible energy in Romanesque stone carving, in architecture, in the creative use of classical motifs as well as in the First Crusade. He notes the sudden emergence of the cult of the Virgin Mary, speculating that it might be the result of Byzantine or Middle Eastern influences.

3. Romance and Reality
directed by Michael Gill
tx 9 March 1969

The chivalric world of princely courts in the 14th and 15th centuries: a world full of delights such as the Unicorn Tapestries and the *Très Riches Heures* of the Duc de Berry, albeit one Clark finds somewhat indulgent. Politeness and *douceur de vivre* may be fruits of civilisation, but are not synonymous with it. He considers the life and teachings of St Francis of Assisi, chivalrous knight turned worshipper of nature, before addressing Giotto and his Arena Chapel frescoes.

4. Man: The Measure of All Things
directed by Ann Turner
tx 16 March 1969

The fifteenth-century Renaissance leads Clark to consider the discovery of perspective as well as of portraiture's potential to convey personality. He considers the different environments in which human creativity can flourish, such as cities and courts. Urbino is presented as the most civilised Renaissance court. Clark nonetheless looks beyond the city's walls to consider what role the peasantry and countryside can and do play in narratives of civilisation.

5. The Hero as Artist
directed by Michael Gill
tx 23 March 1969

How papal patronage of Raphael, Michelangelo and Leonardo Da Vinci in the early 15th century acted as a catalyst for the most concentrated outburst of artistic creativity in European history. Michelangelo's *Prisoners* and pages from Da Vinci's notebooks are the focus of extended sequences. Clark nonetheless points out the 'deadening influence' Raphael's surfeit of perfectly toned supermen had on art in the centuries that follow, and struggles to locate Leonardo's genius in the Renaissance as a whole. We are left with two different yet equally unsatisfactory alternatives: man as immortal god, or man as mechanism.

6. Protest and Communication
directed by Peter Montagnon
tx 30 March 1969

'What went wrong with that solid-looking world?' Clark seeks to trace the origins of the orgy of violence unleashed by the Reformation of sixteenth-century Germany and the Low Countries. This is partly blamed on the latent passions of the Germans, as revealed in the carving of Riemenschneider and the woodcuts of Dürer. Clark demonstrates a printing press in Antwerp, and follows the wanderings of Erasmus and Luther before joining Montaigne in his tower. He finds echoes of the essayist in a series of costumed scenes from Shakespeare's *King Lear* and *Hamlet*, which bring the episode to an ambiguous end.

7. Grandeur and Obedience
directed by Peter Montagnon
tx 6 April 1969

Returning to Rome of the later 15th century, Clark shows how the Roman Catholic church harnessed the talents of sculptors such as Bernini to promote the Counter-Reformation across southern Europe. He dwells lovingly on Bernini's *Apollo and Daphne* but cannot help feeling that baroque art got out of control. Like the cinema of the 1920s to which it is compared, such works threaten to over-indulge their illusionary and exploitative aspects. 'The stopper is out', and the residue of true art will soon evaporate.

8. The Light of Experience
directed by Michael Gill
tx 13 April 1969

Lush sounds and opulent interiors give way to light, observation and stillness as Clark moves to consider seventeenth-century Holland and England. He seeks to defend the bourgeois capitalist citizens of Amsterdam from the condescension and hostility of the Marxists of his own time – they are individuals coming together for a public purpose. Clark notes significant scientific and philosophical advances by the likes of Descartes, Wren and the Royal Society, and relishes the degree to which art and science had yet to grow apart. However 'progressive' it may have seemed, the subsequent solitary path chosen by science has not furthered civilisation.

9. The Pursuit of Happiness
directed by Peter Montagnon
tx 20 April 1969

Clark dutifully covers the French classicist architecture of the Louvre before diving into the 'rococo sea', where the music of Handel and Mozart and paintings of Watteau swirl around the architecture of Balthasar Neumann. This civilised moment recognised a new truth about pleasure: it is transitory, and therefore something quite serious. The music of Mozart shows a figure with one foot in this happy, loving world, and one in a very different age. The hero of *Don Giovanni* looks forward to the revolutionary world of episode 12.

149

10. The Smile of Reason
directed by Michael Gill
tx 27 April 1969

Staying in the 18th century, Clark considers how the *salons* of Paris, the campaigns of Voltaire and the still-lives of Chardin managed to champion enduring human rights and develop a new, frequently sceptical perspective on our world without dispensing with belief and without challenging the inequalities that underpinned their society. Jefferson and Washington carry these ideas to the New World. Clark challenges us to ask why we find the real charms of pre-1789 Europe repellent, and points out the 'different sorts of exploitation' that underpin our own society.

11. The Worship of Nature
directed by Peter Montagnon and Ann Turner
tx 4 May 1969

Opening in the pastoral idyll of the Lake District, Clark shows how eighteenth-century poets and painters found in the cult of nature both a mirror of the human soul and a replacement for religion. The shallow effusions of minor poets such

as Collins gradually become wider in scope and deeper in sentiment until they debouch in the *Confessions* of Jean-Jacques Rousseau. The poetry of Goethe, cloudscapes of Constable and pure colour of Turner's landscapes raise man's response to the natural world to new heights of sensation, which in Turner's case anticipate the Impressionist movement of fifty years later. Sitting in a boat on the lake next to Rousseau's home, Clark muses on whether the pursuit of sensation might not have gone too far.

12. The Fallacies of Hope
directed by Michael Gill
tx 11 May 1969

Summoned by 'the infinite', Clark leaves the ordered world of an eighteenth-century Neo-Palladian interior behind. We are embarked with Beethoven, Byron, Rodin and others on a perilous voyage to new horizons of conquest, which forever retreat from us. Looking out over the would-be revolutionaries of 1968 Paris, Clark is reminded of all the hopes successive revolutions have raised since 1789: inarticulate hopes, yet

nonetheless dashed. As Rodin's *Burghers of Calais* intimates, we are almost numbed by these disappointments. Rodin's *Monument to Balzac* inspires in Clark new hope, however, that we can tackle and defeat all the forces that threaten to impair humanity.

13. Heroic Materialism
directed by Michael Gill
tx 18 May 1969

The New York skyline finds Clark musing on the changes wrought by the Industrial Revolution, whose brutalising effects manifested themselves in a curious counterpoint with the discovery of humanitarian impulses towards groups of people whose fate had previously been totally ignored. Steam locomotives, Renoir, Van Gogh and Einstein are all discussed, leaving us with '*no idea where we are going*'. For all the menace of atomic warfare, Clark draws solace from new universities and their students – and from his personal creed, which he now delivers. Marxism has failed, and Heroic Materialism is not enough, Clark concludes. We are left to recognise the true path.

Index

Page numbers in *italics* refer to illustrations.

153

List of Illustrations

Images from *Civilisation*, BBC; pp. 28, 112, © Tate, London 2008; p. 30 – *Elgar*, BBC; p. 32 – *Francis Bacon: Fragments of a Portrait*, BBC; p. 33 – *The Peaches*, BFI Experimental Film Fund; p. 35 – *The Glory That Was Greece*, BBC; p. 40 – *The Royal Palaces of Britain*, BBC/ITV; p. 71 – *The Ascent of Man*, BBC TV/Time-Life Films; pp. 103, 127, courtesy of the National Public Broadcasting Archives, University of Maryland; pp. 105, 108, 117, courtesy of the Board of Trustees, National Gallery of Art, Washington; p. 121 – *The Secret Life of Paintings*, BBC; pp. 123, 130 – *Simon Schama's Power of Art*, BBC Specialist Factual; p. 129 – *How Art Made the World*, © Community Television of Southern California; p. 134 – *Ways of Seeing*, © BBC; p. 135 – *The Shock of the New*, BBC; p. 139 – *This Is Civilisation*, Seneca Productions.

Also Published:
